Take Time To Notice II
&
The Silver Lining

Take Time To Notice II
&
The Silver Lining

Joni Carol

Take Time To Notice II
& The Silver Lining

Joni Carol

ISBN: 1-932205-07-1

Library of Congress Catalog Control Number: 2002117029

Word Association Publishers
205 Fifth Avenue
Tarentum, Pennsylvania 15084
800-827-7903
www.wordassociation.com

**"Take Time To Notice" is also a song available on CD with lyrics by
Joni Carol, performed by Deana Muro**

Someone above has sunshine he's addressing
Can we number your blessings?
Family ties, sunshine, apple pie, being alive
No matter where or when you begin, just ask and he'll stop in

Take time to notice, take time to care
Do everything beautifully and make people aware
Your sun can be my sun, For many days I have none
I know you're not the only one

Find it in your heart to do a humanitarian deed
Tomorrow you'll see what has grown from that seed
Please remember to honor Mom and Dad
Even though you'd rather not bother 'cause you may be feeling mad

Just take time to notice, take time to care
Do everything beautifully and make someone aware
My sun can be your sun, for all those days when you have none
Our lord knows you're not the only one

There is beauty abound for your senses to behold
Smell the flowers, watch the animals, and sunrise so bold
Imagine what life would be like if you didn't need anyone
Your heart would not be warmed by someone else's sun

Take time to notice, take time to care
Do everything so beautifully that you'll make people aware
Your sun can be my sun, for all those days when I'll have none
I know you're not the only one

Take time to notice, take time to care
Do everything beautifully and make people aware
My sun can be your sun, for many days I had none
Carol knows you're not the only one

Just take time

Introduction

To all who read this:

As my family and I watched our mother struggle for her life during her protracted hospital stay, I was blessed with the ability to still look around us through the daily dismal prognosis and find some ray of hope. Everyday for five months, to the hospital I would go. Many days turned into nights as I would sleep in her room, some nights even in her bed. Twice we were instructed to call in clergy, as she was "just not going to make it." They could no longer sustain her. She did not know my sister and me for over a year even though we rarely left her side.

I kept a daily journal of all details during her illness and at night, as I wrote, I would search deeply to find something positive from the day. Every thought in this book is from my own experiences and personal struggle.

This is the end product which evolved from what I reflected on each day for survival. I now want you to take time to notice that the sun will always come up eventually; not always from the same place and not always full sun, but if you believe in a cause and hold tight to your faith, the sun will not let you down.

It has been almost three years. My mother is now recovering at home. She still needs 24 hour supervision and companionship, but the woman who was practically brain-dead for months and supposedly had her speech center totally destroyed from a severe hemorrhage can now tell you, "Methuselah is the oldest man in the Bible!" So, chin up and look around! There is still a lot of good in our world.

Sincerely,
Joni Carol

A Gift for _____

From:
Your ray of sunshine _____

Table of Contents

Chapters

1 *Humanitarian Aid* *1*

2 *Honor thy mother and father.* *14*

3 *God is Great, God is Good* *21*

4 *The Funny Bone* *31*

5 *The Wonders of Nature.* *44*

6 *Imagine That.* *55*

Special credits to:

Delby Kolodziej, Mark Kolodziej, Shawna Kolodziej, Kelley R. Kolodziej, Isaac and Kimberly Lanham, Jeri McClinton, Paul McGinty, Tom Amati, Joanne Bowden, Catherine Suzich, Rodney and Joan Smith, Tracy L. Tracy, Norma Normandy, Jean Kohut, Rev. Pam Hudson, Terri Hudson, Tom and Audrey Franzetta, Don and Karen Koger, Rose Koger, Blair and Bea Smith, Deane and Stephanie Smith, the Charletta Families, Arthur Monack, the late Joe DeStefano, Franci Lucas, Pat Taylor, Pattie Kail, David Mendicino, Chris Zewe, Nancy Zoror, Margie Goodrum, Chuck and Suzanne Venneri, Linda Ciappa, Kathy Cossell, Denise Mornak, Jack Ladesic, Celia Jayakumar, the Muro Family, June Popio, Art Turner, Barbara Bonde, Carole Wilcox, Janice Fretz, The Greenery Rehabilitation Center, and Fells Methodist Church.

Special Thanks

Thank you to all the angels sent to push away the clouds and let an eclipsed sun shine in our lives.

Mary Weaver, Minnie Sala, Craig Rice, and Pastor Marlin Miller

Thank you to the rest of my family both near and far. And a special thanks to my boyfriend, Johnny, who stuck beside me and gave me the moral support I needed no matter how ill-tempered I became at times.

Introduction: Humanitarian Aid

Humanitarian aid comes in many forms and plays a starring role in peoples' lives if you take the time to look around. There are always people willing to give up their Saturdays to stand in front of your local grocery store to collect for the March of Dimes, Easter Seals, Salvation Army, etc...   I personally love to see when neighbors, who don't normally have time to socialize, band together during crises such as floods, fires, hurricanes. . .

I have a special story to share about my personal savior as far as humanitarian aid. I have a girlfriend who has been my friend since first grade. That is almost 40 years. Her name is Tracy. Tracy was always a very headstrong and independent person. She was the first in our circle of friends to have a real boyfriend, a car, and a job. When she turned 35 she was diagnosed with an aggressive form of multiple sclerosis. Within a year, she was confined to a wheelchair. Tracy

1

seemed to go directly to the acceptance stage of her disease. She was never one to lie around crying, "Why me?" Instead, she just adapted and said, "Okay, what do I do now?" Her entire life is one constant struggle with all the expected M.S. side effects plus an acute attack of pancreatitis which almost cost her life. Tracy can't walk a step, but she still drives and lives a full life nevertheless. She goes water skiing, takes care of her lawn on her riding lawnmower, and is active with the M.S. association. As you can imagine, Tracy has set an example for me time and again of how to be strong and enduring. She has given me humanitarian aid over and over throughout my mother's illness. I'd find myself complaining to her in despair about mother's paralyzed leg and how she may never be able to walk again at age 66. There would be Tracy empathizing with me and crying herself for my mother's sake. She accepts her condition so well I tend to forget she's been crippled for almost 10 years! When Tracy would sense that I was exhausted juggling my job and going back and forth to the hospital, she'd say, "If someone could meet me at the hospital to help

me get into my wheelchair, I'll sit with your mother all day," or "If one of her sitters at home needs a ride, I'll pick them up." Everytime I start feeling sorry for myself, her smiling face pops up in my mind, and I know I can go on.

I just want you to know, Tracy, your friendship is priceless, and I thank you.

Humanitarian Aid

Take Time To Notice:

How the more you do for others, the more you want to do.

How, when you are so desperately in need, you want to help others in need.

How people are very helpful when you're with someone in a wheelchair.

How important it is to tell someone they're doing a good job.

How people who have experienced your similar pain really <u>DO</u> understand.

How good it feels to tell someone they look nice when you're thinking it rather than keeping it to yourself.

Take Time To Notice:

How everyone deals with stress differently; we must remember to be understanding.

How happy you can make your little neighbor lady by just helping her with the grocery bags.

How mankind still comes through for one another during times of crises.

How many people still do charity work.

How you'll never miss something if you give it to someone who needs it more than you do.

How people who care, can tell when you are not yourself.

How good it feels to give someone a true compliment without envy.

How during times of dire heartache any change can be a relief.

Take Time To Notice:

How important a touch is to someone frightened.

How nursing homes offer so many activities to their residents.

How, when you open your heart to love and compassion, you put your own wants and needs aside. Then you can gain tremendous power to keep going for someone else

How, if you spend enough time with someone who has a severe speech defect, you begin to understand him or her.

How reading a story to the elderly has a calming effect, just as if they were five years old again.

How when you give a piece of your heart, the heart seems to grow larger and larger; therefore, there is always more love where that came from. Whereas, many who self-indulge with material things wonder: "Is that all there is?"

Take Time To Notice:

How so many people all around us could sure use just a drop of love. For there is...

No shoulder too big to embrace.
No tear too wet to dry.
No wound too deep to heal.
No heart too cold to touch.
No soul too dim to brighten.

Some people will always be caregivers. As youngsters some of you are taught to look after a younger brother or sister. Then you have children of your own and just as you get finished raising your children, you care for your grandchildren. Then after that, many times you get called upon to care for an aging parent. Then, hopefully, life goes full circle and someone is there to tend to your needs. I just believe that we are to be there to do our best at whatever God puts before us.

How many people are organ donors.

Take Time To Notice:

How the overuse and abuse of drugs is so prevalent in today's society. The only way I can empathize with it is to consider drug addiction as an illness just like cancer or AIDS. There certainly are enough people out there trying to understand and remedy this epidemic. But, just like any cure, some patients respond better to treatment than others.

How music has the power to totally change your mood. Even when Mom was in a semi-coma, something called global aphasia, we bought her a tape with one of her favorite songs, Wooly Bully. We put a headset on her to play the song and she spontaneously started bobbing her head and tapped her extremities to the best of her ability to the beat of the music. Keep in mind, this was at a time when she barely responded to painful stimulation.

That there is such a silver lining when you have earned peace in your heart. After someone is gone for good from this existence, you, too, will have that peace when you are certain you did all you could.

8

Take Time To Notice:

How former drug addicts make the best counselors in that field.

How wonderful it is that there's a support group out there for whatever ails you.

How though we are given inalienable rights with: "Life, Liberty and The Pursuit of Happiness," what good are they if we are selfish with them? What good is life if you only care about your life? Liberty is dangerous if you take your freedoms too far and impinge upon others freedoms. What gratification is there in happiness if it counteracts someone else's happiness?

How the nine bodily systems are not only functions to enhance your life, but you may lend their worth to anyone and everyone's system.
    Skeletal System: To lift someone.
    Respiratory System: To learn CPR
    Reproductive System: To give life
    Circulatory System: To donate blood
    Endocrine System: To labor hard and sweat for someone else's benefit

Neurologic System: To think of solutions for someone else's problems
Muscular System: To strengthen someone
Digestive System: To share a meal with someone
Integumentary System: To touch someone

How those who are self-absorbed have such an unsatisfied neediness that it clouds their ability to notice others' needs. Then, one day, they by chance lend a hand to someone and suddenly realize how good it feels. People are capable of change, but we can't force their changes simply by asking. Everyone grows differently and we continue to go through growth spurts even as adults.

How, when you give from the heart to someone in need, you don't realize right at that very moment how he or she is actually enriching your life.

Take Time To Notice:

How medicine, though highly technical, is still basic mechanics, carpentry, and plumbing: a bypass and a replacement here, a repair or an unclogging there. Let's make something larger, smaller, straighter or remove it all together. Then drain some fluid or maybe pump some back in... What remains the most important is still the human factor. Along with having the proper skills, one must have love in the heart and the desire to want everyone touched to walk away a better person.

How difficult it is to buy someone a gift these days. This is usually because people already have just about everything they could possibly need...we all could get by with a whole lot less. Wouldn't it feel great to buy someone a winter coat simply because they don't have one?

How it is still a major priority to give your most beloved one a Christmas gift, even though they may be in a coma. Sounds pointless, but it happens.

Take Time To Notice:

How when you ask a true friend for a favor, he or she will spontaneously say "Sure" instead of "What is it?"

How we can learn something from everyone who crosses our paths.

How even though we may at times think we need no one, we even tout ourselves as being "Loners." When we do need to get the job done we are helpless without some assistance from mankind.

How when our lives are entangled in the needs of someone else's life, the trials seem insurmountable at that time. No matter how difficult then, once you improve their quality of life, looking back will only be beautiful.

How our doctors today study so long and hard to specialize in a particular field. Our bodies are so intricate with specific needs. Doctors now are able to better understand just how complex and individual we are.

12

Take Time To Notice:

How we have the ability to not only allow sunshine into our lives but also the capability to let some out of our lives. You can be someone else's sunshine any day of the year. You have 365 to choose from.

…that if you are fortunate enough to have anything nice, you must be prepared to take care of it to keep it that way. If you have a beautiful flowerbed or a vegetable garden, you must take care of them. A pretty lawn requires much maintenance. With a brand new pair of leather shoes, they'll look old and worn before you know it if you don't keep them clean and polished. It is so nice to buy new furniture, but if you abuse it soon you'll be covering it up to hide all the stains you've been careless enough to cause. Just as, if you are blessed to have a wonderful spouse, children, or nice friends, be prepared to take care of them.

How doing for others is just like any other skill, the more you do it, the better you become at it.

Introduction: Honor Thy Mother and Father

The nineties, like all decades, had certain catch phrases. One of them was "dysfunctional family." My family is no exception. We four children span only a five year age difference from oldest to youngest. We all have a deep unspoken love for one another. Our father became a father prematurely in his life. I now realize he just wasn't cut out to be the perfect dad at age 20. Parenthood does not suit everyone. It's like saying every man has to be a doctor or rocket scientist when he grows up. Like many fathers of that era, mine knew only that he was supposed to be a financial provider. He knew not what activities we children were involved in at school or even how well we were doing with our studies. Nevertheless, our mother was left to run with the ball and she managed to give us everything from nothing. Looking back now, I see a bold delineation between mother's daily life and

14

father's. This dichotomy seemed to stay intact to some degree throughout their marriage, that is, up until mother's catastrophe.

When we opted to take our mother home from the nursing home to care for her, I had several major concerns. She was discharged with a feeding tube, and she was incontinent. My sister and I were with her day and night for 100 days at the home, so we figured it may be good therapy for all of us to be in her own home. We were willing to learn how to operate the feeding pump, we were instructed how to react in case of a seizure, and we'd have more hands-on control of her "potty training." More than these challenges, I was overcome with worry about how my father would react. Would he be patient? Would he be understanding and helpful? He was definitely remiss in the nurturing, affectionate departments and quite frankly hadn't had much practice.

I prayed to God, "Please help my father to open his heart to love and compassion. We need him on our side. He's not well himself and his life has been turned upside down." Guess what? It is such a delight to see my mother and father sitting side by side, holding hands and

kissing many times a day. They even went to church and renewed their wedding vows. It all came naturally to my father. He helps care for her, buys her more cards than he ever did, and has not complained once about the daily chaos and money being spent for her around-the-clock care. One day my mother said to him, "Pappy, are you going to leave me?" He responded: "Carol, I married you for better, for worse, in sickness and in health, till death do we part." I knew my prayers had been answered at that moment.

Honor Thy Mother and Father

Take Time To Notice:

Your mother's hands, handwriting, and her smile; this way you'll have them forever.

Your father's frown lines and hairline; they may be just like yours.

What kind of daily pills your loved ones take and why.

How many people still visit cemeteries on Memorial Day.

How many parents today are involved with their children's sports activities.

How most families really do <u>want</u> to be family oriented; it just doesn't always work out that way.

Take Time To Notice:

How even the hardest of hearts crumble when they see their loved one suffering.

How, when you watch someone you deeply love suffer, it is one of the few times you'll wish your life away - six months, maybe a year at a time - in hopes that "maybe by then, they'll be better."

How you can learn invaluable pearls of wisdom from your elders.

How we always want our parents' approval no matter how old we are.

How important it is to our parents to sit on the back porch with them and not appear to be in any hurry.

How most everything has no significance when a loved one is ill.

How touching it is to discover your parents still carry old pictures of you in their wallets.

Take Time To Notice:

How almost every trait you possess is an inherited hand-me-down characteristic from either your mother or your father.

How just after you've gone through that age where it's "uncool" to hang out with your parents, you start liking them better.

How mothers have this built-in self-sacrificing mechanism. She not only gives you birth but she feels obligated to sacrifice for you until she physically has no more to give.

How as we grow older we definitely do a role reversal with our parents. Just as they did for us as children, we must be patient. Don't raise our voices, explain everything in plain, explicit detail, and be sure to compliment them on any menial project.

How we may at times notice undesirable character traits in our parents, but still we readily accept them for being that way. Even though we may not agree with them, we just kind of hope

19

that little fault doesn't manifest itself in our personality some day! P.S. I think it's called respect.

How your loved ones like their coffee or tea. Mom and dad will especially feel honored.

How comforting it is to fall asleep, as an adult, while holding your mother's hand.

Introduction: God is Great, God is Good

As you can imagine, during my mother's critical illness, I suffered many sleepless nights. I slept at the hospital when I could. When I slept at home, I would toss and turn in my bed and call the intensive care unit every 3-4 hours. One night as I lay there crying, I felt unusually distraught. I clutched my mother's picture close to me, as I generally slept with it in my bed. I had such uncontrollable pain and nausea. I genuinely felt a sharp steady pain from my head to my toes; my insides were on fire and I was trembling out of control. I thought maybe I was about to die. What else could feel so awful? I believe now, since I am an extension of my mother, it was a natural impulse that I was suffering because she was. This particular night I almost felt possessed. I was unable to reason things out. All I knew was that my heart was broken, and this wreaked punishment over my

entire body. I prayed so desperately, "God, please help me, let me know somehow, someway, that everything will be all right." Then as I opened my swollen, teary eyes, I saw a bright and glowing arc of light across my bedroom ceiling. It spanned from the far wall on my left up and over my bed and extended on an angle to the corner where my door is. It even appeared to have a tiny, misty- like spray emitting from it. I kept blinking to see if it would disappear, but it didn't. Then I looked all around the darkened perimeters of my room to determine if maybe some light was beaming in from a crack around the windows or the door. There was no light source to explain this sudden ray of light.....almost like a rainbow without the different colors. After that I knew God was watching over me. I noticed a gentle calming and peacefully went to sleep.

God is Great, God is Good

Take Time To Notice:

How, even when you feel the whole world is against you, you're able to find at least one angel among the crowd to comfort you.

How the Bible still remains the #1 Best Seller.

How God puts wonderful people in our paths when we need them most.

How you have to be really down at some point in life to realize how great being up feels. I have finally figured out what Jesus meant when he said, "Blessed are the poor in spirit." Matthew Chapter 5:3

How our family priests, preachers, and ministers find so many extra hours in their day to visit us when we need them, and they always know just what to say.

Take Time To Notice:

How, when we are really desperate for answers to our dilemmas, we look for signs from anywhere. We hope for an ultimate power. The answers don't come and ring our doorbells, but they do come.

How, when we go through these traumatic events in life, we draw strength from unusual sources, some commonly understandable, some camouflaged golden nuggets. A few of my lifesavers were:

The Serenity Prayer

Psalms 23

Phillipians 4:13

And this one from an unknown source: "I'm not okay and you're not okay, but that's ok!"

How human hands are far too awkward to open the petals of a rose bud; it blossoms only by God's warm sunshine and falling rain.

How children with Down's Syndrome are so happy and loving.

Take Time To Notice:

How you may at times find yourself praying for the silliest things like, say, a parking space, when you're in a hurry and presto!

How we are all given certain innate traits at birth. Persistence, for example, is one that we exercise as infants. We attempt to walk. We repeatedly fall down, but get back up and try, try again. As we grow older, we are granted the inalienable right to continue using our persistence tool. Again, we have a choice as an adult: we can hold tight to our God-given gift or allow it to become lame.

How when we watch our beloved ones suffer, we pray... we pray so hard: please let them recover, please heal them. God has an ultimate plan, and it's not the same for everyone. Some of us He keeps here to carry on business on earth. Then, sometimes perhaps, he needs more good people to help him up in heaven. It is not easy, but there comes a time when we must let go and say, "Go ahead, be with God ; I'll be all right."

Take Time To Notice:

How God knew spreading sunshine around was of utmost importance. Why else would he dedicate that job to day #1? "Let there be light." Genesis Chapter I.

How those with no faith grow bitter during a tragedy and those with a strong faith grow stronger.

How we all have so many irrevocable choices each day. You decide which ones seem more appealing. Would you prefer to be remembered for your Kindness or Rudeness? Loyalty or Betrayal? Acceptance or Resentment?

How the words we say DO matter. The tongue is very likely the most powerful part of the body; it can scar someone for life. It has the ability to make friends or enemies, to make someone laugh or cry. It is our God-given tool and we can choose to produce all good if we like. As James Chapter 3 tells us: "A fountain does not allow both bitter and sweet water to flow from it."

Take Time To Notice:

How we could all benefit from reviewing the seven cardinal sins and targeting the one or ones where we need the most discipline. I personally, find myself embracing the need to steer clear of pride, greed, and envy.

How many of us are still smitten with the age old question of "Why is there so much human suffering?" I suppose we will find out some day, but for now, a friend of mine made me realize we probably suffer because God suffers. He loves us so much that He hurts when we hurt, and He grieves when we sin. He holds life in such synchronistic balance that we must experience sorrow to appreciate laughter and we must experience sickness to appreciate health. We cannot attempt to understand His decisions with our human logic. Remember we use only 10% of our brains.

There is such an unfathomable difference between God and us, that by comparison, the dissimilarity between our neighbor and us is miniscule.

Take Time To Notice:

How becoming best friends with God can be a lifelong process. I work at it daily. I'm not exactly where I want to be, but at least I'm not where I used to be.

How everyone as a skeleton would look alike. God adorned our bodies with flesh, hair, pretty eye colors and various other traits to make us "us"! He could have left us unsightly with only bones, but He didn't. I believe it's okay to decorate our bodily temples with pretty clothes, make-up, etc. After all, He started the trend. I believe He wants us to look pleasing to each other as long as we don't become obsessed with it. Remember, everything in moderation.

How it is so ironic when you find God, He has a way of surrounding you with His dutiful servants. A silver lining for me has been; having God as my friend has led me to the front doors of many friends of God.

And remember the next time you become really angry with someone that no matter what, God loves us all the same.

Take Time To Notice:

How if you were to take the back off a clock you would see such fine craftsmanship. One gear moving another to synchronize movement of maybe a tiny belt or spring all in an effort to keep perfect time. How does this occur? Because someone took the time to design this. How can anyone examine even a minor function of our human bodies and not realize that someone designed them? Creations of this magnitude could not just happen without a mastermind behind them.

How God could have created our world to be completely boring to taste, to look at, to communicate with and to smell. But, He didn't, did He?

Even when all your strengths may seem depleted, you'll always have the power of prayer

When we are in dire distress it seems all we can do is pray. What do those with no faith do in their time of need?

Take Time To Notice:

How God is always patiently waiting to be invited into our lives. Although He doesn't force Himself in, He is undoubtedly receptive to our asking no matter how long it takes. Even if it takes some the better part of our lives, He doesn't get an attitude and say; "Never mind now; I've been waiting 40 years for you"!

Introduction: "The Funny Bone"

During the earlier stages of my mother's recovery, she developed her very own language. She articulated well but had an extremely colorful vocabulary. All she wanted was "the red and the green." She wondered where her "stumperdowny" had gone, and could she please have another "kineejer?"

Even though our long days were filled mainly with heartache and tears, those conversations made my sister and me realize it was okay to laugh. The levity was good for our minds and souls and a nice distraction from all the serious decision-making we had to do. Laughter is a gift we are all given and it has no language barriers.

Now we shall fast forward to Mother's recovery years later. Her speaking skills improved intermittently but steadily enough for us to realize hope. Her speech remained clear and she retained a wide vocabulary, but her brain was kind of like a junk drawer. Everything

she needed was in there, but many times, she couldn't find what she was looking for. Fortunately, she never lost her sense of humor and she still enjoyed laughing at herself. One morning in particular when she awakened my sister for help getting to the potty for her a.m. visit, Janie asked her if she wanted to get up for the day. Mummy, still obviously desiring more sleep, said, "No, just put me back in the drawer." Then there was the time I made the mistake of sitting mummy on her potty chair with the lid still down and she immediately let me know by blurting out, "Joni, I'm not hanging right!" Then another time she observed Janie putting our family dog, Tessa, outside on her chain as was standard procedure. Then, Janie proceeded to let her own dog, Dane, out running freely. Well, Mummy got very upset that Janie just left Dane "go outside plain!" Oh those precious moments of hearing her laugh when she'd realize the funny things that came out of her mouth...Like the time she meant to tell me she was hungry for a hamburger, but told me she wanted a liver sandwich with applesauce on it instead.

The Funny Bone

Take Time To Notice:

How, when you sing a happy song, it's impossible to be sad!

How certain people can make you laugh no matter what.

How, when you want some material thing, it loses its sacredness after you've obtained it, and then you just move on to yearning for something else.

How, no matter who you'd ask, they say, "Yes, I'm a good person." It's nice to know at least everyone WANTS to be good.

How people really don't care if your house is clean. They just want to feel welcome.

How many homeless people really don't look like they're underfed!

Take Time To Notice:

How senior citizens can freely joke with one another about getting old.

How the older one gets, the less fear one has of dying.

How much you've transformed into your mother or father without even trying.

How, when every minute of your day is dedicated to one demanding cause, you wonder what everyone else could possibly be doing with all their time.

How, when you are tortured day in and day out with your seemingly unending burden, you wonder how others around you could have the nerve to be happy and laughing.

How our cars become our very faithful friends when we are swept up in a non-stop whirlwind crisis. Besides offering us the transportation to desperately arrive at our destination, they can console us with music, lend a back seat to serve as storage for

tomorrow's outfit, and gladly offer a dining area right there at the wheel.

How strangers still want to get to know us. They'll find you on a plane, in a waiting room, or on vacation when you thought you were striving to get away from it all!

How, when you're feeling gloomy on a rainy day, you'll always find someone who says, "Well, we need the rain."

How certain things cannot be improved upon: a coke is a coke whether Bill Gates buys one or your local newspaper boy buys one.

How much variety with everything we have around us. You can go to a major chain video store with thousands of movies to rent and still find people roaming around unable to make a selection.

How, when your precious time is so limited, you get very adept at doing multiple chores at the same time. For instance, brushing your teeth while going to the bathroom, painting your

35

Take Time To Notice:

fingernails while talking on the phone, or applying make-up while driving.

How laughter sounds and means the same thing no matter what language one speaks.

How we've never seen the back of our own heads. Thank goodness for mirrors and photographs, or we'd never really know what we look like.

How we are all given sort of package deals within ourselves. All in all, it seems they are generally fair. Everyone is blessed with certain gifts and redeemable qualities...take time to notice how we all age differently. Some of us grey prematurely, some of us get deep facial lines at a younger age, but notice, usually you can't have both. Some of us lose our teeth at a certain age while others lose their hair; most of the time, you can't have both. There are those of us who get paunchy about the stomach, and possibly large around the back with flabby arms, then others tend to get thicker through the leg and hip area. The nice thing is most often, you can't have both. Notice our extremities, hands

for example: some of us have hands that reflect every past minute of hard work with weathered, dry, and cracked skin. Whereas some feet grow all those knobby things. Lucky for us that generally you can't have both. Some of us are blessed with only those breath-taking eyes that project peace and acceptance inside because we realize we are special no matter what.

How as we age, many things just take longer, like shaving for example. We women find it is much more difficult to shave under our arms. There are all these hard to reach valleys in our arm pits that never existed before. For you men, shaving your faces has never-ending barriers, you seem to start at your shoulders, up the neck, past and including the nostrils, maybe snip off a long straggler at the eyebrows then back past and into the ears.

That if you're unsure how to be a good friend, ask your pet! They have some excellent instincts. Dogs, I know, are very predictable. They always greet you the same way. You don't have to tip toe around them some days wondering why they are mad at you. If they fall, they may let out a yelp, but they quickly come to you for comfort rather than looking for a reason to blame you.

Take Time To Notice:

How as we age, we have no control over the metamorphic changes our bodies go through... some features that we wish would stay small, get larger, while other features we'd prefer stay large and full, shrink away to nothing. It is a known fact that the nose and the ears never stop growing throughout life; they become fuller, thickened and elongated. Whereas, our lips, eyelids, and buttocks (es) slide, droop, and wither away.

How we abbreviate our language. For instance, if you are maybe a CEO or a VP of say GM or 3M, you might talk to your CPA about an IRA or a CD so that the IRS doesn't take as much when you get your W-2. Or perhaps if you're an MD or an RN you have to deal with the ER ,the OR, the ICU and the NICU. You must monitor your patients' IV and BP and tend to them in the case of a UTI, an MI or a TIA. Then we have the really prestigious VIP's in the USA that head the CIA, the FBI, the FDA and the FAA. Let's just hope they're using their high IQ's and great QPA's on the job rather than in front of the TV watching MTV or a DVD, or using their PC's to track AT&T, MCI, or IBM on AOL. One more thing, please show proper ID

if the LAPD pulls over your VW, RV or SUV. Remember a DUI gets you nowhere except to AA or a DOA. Think instead of that someone in your life who deserves an RSVP for all their TLC! S.W.A.K. www.com xoxoxoxo

How we have only one mouth to talk with but two ears to listen with...listen twice as much as you talk.

We have only one behind to sit on yet two legs to walk with...walk twice as much as you sit.

We have two eyes to cry with but 32 teeth to show off when we smile...smile at least twice as much as you cry.

We have only one back to turn to someone and two hands and arms to help them with. Help them and hug them rather than walk away from them.

How its nice to know a handful of things are still kept simple, such as a paper clip, a dust pan, a salt shaker, and a rubber band. No instructions required!

How we can see everything in life from a distance and from different angles-except ourselves.

Take Time To Notice:

How our English dictionaries are at least twice the size of foreign language dictionaries. Do you think maybe we talk too much?

How sometimes we choose to disregard instructions for assembling or using gadgets and equipment. We fumble through trying to make sense of all the pieces, just as we all, at times, fudge our way through life's experiences. The Bible, our personal manual, has everything in it we need to know, but still we ignore our handy guide book and try to make sense of all the pieces.

When you finally do get "caught up" it's just for that day. Tomorrow you get to do it all over again!

How very gratifying it is to learn something new about yourself. I don't like waking up in the middle of the night, but I love waking up in the middle of the day!!

Take Time To Notice:

How some people constantly complain! Not only are their glasses half empty, but their partly sunny days are instead partly cloudy. These complainers are consumed with trying to convince others their lives are far worse than everyone else's. Fortunately, I have found these people to be at least a "semi-rare" breed. Most people have unbelievable strength reserves; physically, spiritually and emotionally. I have deduced that what these poor weak souls thirst for is pity and recognition. I've decided, "What the heck." We might as well supply them with what they thrive on. Just feel blessed that you're not one of them!

How when we are young we get so excited with excitement. When we are older we get so comfortable with comfort.

How our society focuses so much on our personal gratification. We definitely suffer from the "me" syndrome. "I'm stressed." "I need a break." We have so much to be thankful for. In the good ole' days they didn't even measure if they were happy or not or when they last had a vacation. Our ancestors just lived

41

Take Time To Notice:

and made the best of it. If they had cooperative weather to work their fields 16 hours a day for a week straight, they considered themselves lucky!!! Can you imagine your great grandmother sitting around in the afternoon saying "Ya know, I'm just not happy"???

How it seems that 80 percent of the world's doorbells don't work properly. Then what do we do? Resort to our ole' human resources, a knock and a holler!!

The next time you feel all upside-down, remember it is so much better to be downside-up!!!

How so many people buy bottled water at concession stands instead of soft drinks. Twenty years ago if someone would have tried to sell me a bottle of water for a dollar, I would have assumed it was either from the fountain of youth or merely a donation for charity.

42

Take Time To Notice:

How wonderful our lives have become thanks to our ancestors' hard work. They invested so much human interest that even a "stay at home mom" can get a big return in her daily life. Can you fathom your grandmother going out to get her nails done? It is very acceptable in today's society for everyday women to go to the tanning salon, out for a round of golf and then to lunch.

How even skinny people have "fat days"!!!

Introduction: The Wonders of Nature

When my mother went back to the ICU for the second time, her prognosis was 90% mortality. Right around that devastation, two wonderful things were given to me. My boyfriend's Uncle Joe (who would perish within the year himself) gave me a small bottle of blessed holy water. Also, a patient at our office, Monk, went out of his way one day to leave and return with a tiny branch from a tree where there was a supposed sighting of the Blessed Mother. These two men could never have imagined at the time the impact these objects had on my life. They were an utmost important and vital part of my daily routine. I would dab the water on my mother each day trying to concentrate, but use sparingly, on the area of the body which was suffering most at that time. The twig I taped to the family picture on the stand next to her bed. Once a week or so, a leaf would dry up and fall off the branch. When no one was looking, I'd crumble

up part of it and strategically drop pieces in mother's bed. I would save the remaining part of the leaf for another day. After the leaves were gone I'd snap off tiny segments of the branch. I was so frantic one day when I couldn't find her holy water. They had moved her bed and belongings to the isolation section of the ICU. I searched like a quiet lunatic with a pounding heart until I finally found it. That little bottle was definitely my sunshine that day.

The Wonders of Nature

Take Time To Notice:

How all the planets in the universe rotate around the same path, but in their own individual orbits, at their own speeds, and none of them crash into one another.

How dogs are so forgiving.

How our feet, only a fraction the size of our bodies, keep us going even at our worst of times.

How all faces, primarily made up of two eyes, a nose, and a mouth, are basically the same, but with countless variations.

And listen to the birds singing in the morning a few minutes before getting up.

How the sun nourishes all inhabitable life. It works so very hard each day, still it outdoes itself. It makes its grand entrance with a brilliant, bright glow so eager to warm and nurture everything. After a long day it exits even more magnificently. It

46

says goodnight with a spectacular array of evening colors. We should all follow its example as our role model, just like mother used to say, "Rise and shine!"

How people are on a quest to get back to all natural ingredients.

How flowers are so beautiful with their brilliant colors, and no one painted them.

How magnificent trees grow and blossom out in the forest, and no one planted them.

How a simple blossom turns into a juicy fruit or vegetable.

The sun shining through your window. Just pause and absorb it...

The green trees against the blue sky, more beautiful in real life than any photograph.

How a flowing brook rolls on without hesitation not knowing what's ahead.

Take Time To Notice:

How crystal clear water is, despite everything we dump into it.

How many people still plant flowers in the spring.

How many people like things that smell pretty.

How pretty a dandelion is.

How man still has no control of Mother Nature.

How the leaves on the trees tell us when fall is here. We don't need to signal them.

How mental and physical stress causes a great strain on our bodies. We suffer multiple ailments. It feels as though our entire body chemistry is out of balance and will never reverse itself. Yet our bodies are such resilient machines when our lives return to a slow roar; our systems and faces become recognizable again. A miracle occurs, and anguish neutralizes us once more.

48

Take Time To Notice:

How our lives mimic the earth's ecosystem: An event happens which triggers something. Then you meet a new acquaintance, nurture that friendship; many new things thrive on that relationship; new episodes in life grow from that and so on, and so on...

How we cannot create new colors, can't even imagine one!

How laundry hung out on the clothes line still smells better and fresher than anything manufactured and bottled.

How we still love to feel the wind in our hair, the grass under our feet, and the sunshine on our shoulders.

How even clouds have their own personalities. Some time they stand out as bright, white, bubbly individuals. Other days they are lazy and all blended together like a thick grey soup.

How, just as a plant gravitates towards the sun, also do we perk up with the sun: Nature's stimulant!

Take Time To Notice:

How kind Mother Nature can be. She gives us so many natural sedatives. For example: subliminal music to soothe the mind and relax the body are usually recordings of rain falling, ocean waves swishing, or birds singing... Or calm yourself with aromatherapy from chamomile, passion flower and peppermint.

How just as daffodils wait for the spring sunshine to break through the earth and swollen buds await to burst open, our love and souls hunger for that nourishment shed from a sun beam of hope from others.

How even though we are allowed the sun to shine for only part of the day, remember it feels good to share. When our sun goes down, it is shining for someone else on another side of the world.

How blessed we are to be given colors! Colors denote so many emotions. They can be arousing or subduing, bold and exciting or cool and soothing. Would our fruits and vegetables be as tempting had they been created with a grey flesh and charcoal stems and leaves?

Take Time To Notice:

How gratifying it is when things such as flowers or bread baking leave behind wonderful, memorable fragrances. Isn't it nice to know you have that same capability? You can leave behind a pleasant fragrance with the words you say to others. The scent of your kindness will be inhaled and devoured to linger on long after you've gone.

That it is important to be in the sun's beam, but if you try to dominate the sun by staring directly into it, it is blinding. Fortunately, the blindness is temporary for Mother Nature lends various types of sunglasses: A tree, a cloud or a mountain top filters the glare just enough to return you to its glory abound. Becoming a part of the sun and looking just beyond allows us to bask in its many miracles. Just as we should remember: Don't be blinded by your fellow man's faults. Look slightly past the faults to find their halos.

The daylight sun always shines for those with their heads above the clouds.

Take Time To Notice:

How fireplaces used to be incorporated into our homes traditionally as their only heat source. Today many homebuilders still include them. Why? Because no matter how fast paced our lives are we still need to go back to basics for that taste of peace and tranquility. Can you imagine our ancestors actually ordering, buying and having wood delivered already chopped?

The beautiful usually, unseen, hidden world underwater. Just when we think there is too much beauty in our world to comprehend. If ever you've been lucky enough to see what lies beneath the great oceans, you'd see so much more beauty abound. God could have made all the fish the same color and shape. Instead they are all different, brilliantly colored with stripes, spots and iridescent patterns. The species are so numerous no one has ever been able to count them. That is except our Consummate Artist who painted and shaped them all individually.

Take Time To Notice:

How every leaf from every different plant is it's own unique design. One can almost determine the plant variety or even what flower or vegetable it might yield simply by looking at the leaf. Can you come up with a new leaf design, create it, and actually make it grow?

How fruits and vegetables stay plump and healthy while on their vines. However, not long after one falls to the ground if no one is there to catch it, it will soon spoil. Remember, once we fall from our lifelines we too could start to decay.

How many people love animals. They go to zoos just to look at them! We co-habitate with such amazing creatures!

How, try as we may, we simply are not able to make fabrics as beautiful as our Creator can. Just go ahead and attempt to manufacture a feather as lovely as a peacock's, or a fur as luxurious as a tiger's. Then try your hand at some stone as durable and as beautiful as real marble.

Take Time To Notice:

How everything in moderation is always best. Even our most horrendous disasters are okay in small doses. The flickering flame of a candle or a fireplace can be beautiful and mesmerizing to watch. A natural waterfall or a gentle rain can be very calming and a slight breeze through your hair is uplifting and titillating. But, all of these natural wonders are very destructive when there are no boundaries. They teach us that everything needs discipline.

Introduction: "Imagine That"

If you've ever spent much time at a nursing home you'd experience walking away from it with a lot of deep seated sorrow. Many residents there are long forgotten and get little or no company. I had the pleasure of befriending several of the residents at the home where my mother stayed for three months. She was not exactly conscious of what went on around her, so my sister and I spent everyday with her splitting the shifts. A few of the patients would look forward to wheeling their wheelchairs into mother's room knowing we would be there to visit with. Some couldn't get around at all. One resident in particular, "Mikey," was a long-term patient. Mikey didn't get much company, but the staff would take him out to the hallway daily and park him along with all of his cumbersome medical equipment. He was completely paralyzed from the neck down. The only movement I noted was his eyes shifting and a

continuous involuntary twitching jerk about his neck and lower jaw. He seemed to be a total vegetable sitting there with glazed-over eyes staring blankly, while his nourishment relied on a feeding tube, and his every breath relied on a respirator. I passed him several times a day, sometimes with my mother in her wheelchair, and I'd only smile at him. One evening there was an urgent tornado watch. As I listened to the updated report on television, I learned that the tornado was due to touch down right in that very town within 20 minutes. The staff acted promptly, and we managed to move all patients away from the windows in case of any glass breaks. Some patients were put into the hallways, and for some we tried to build makeshift barricades around their beds with mats. Mikey was out in his usual spot. Fortunately, the tornado did not strike at the home that night. After the warning was lifted and everyone was back in bed, I waited around for my mother to fall asleep. I went down to Mikey at the far end of the hall. I decided to talk to him for the first time. I said, "Mikey, everything is ok. The tornado has passed, and everyone is safe." He started

manipulating his mouth more than usual, and after about 15 seconds he finally mustered out, "I was praying." An instant stream of tears ran down my cheeks. Mikey, of all people. There was actually an observant person inside with a thought process. I surmise that he realized there was nothing he could do to help besides pray, so that he did. After that night, I made it a point to talk to Mikey. He always seemed excited to see me and even smiled back then. He would respond to my conversation even though it almost looked painful for him to get a few words out. He would always ask, "How's your mother?" Imagine that....someone as debilitated as Mikey asking how someone else is feeling.

Imagine That

Take Time To Notice:

How we all want so much of everything: A new car, new job, new jewelry, etc. Then when an earthshaking, heartbreaking occurrence happens, it completely disrupts our lives. Suddenly, all we long for is normalcy.

How a good night's sleep makes a new person of you, even if it's only one night out of every three.

How communication devices keep us so much more reachable. Pagers, cell phones, call waiting, answering machines, e-mail, faxes, we must <u>want</u> to stay in touch?

How hospitals no longer use overhead paging systems. Everyone wears a pager (or two or three).

How good it feels to get into your own nice cozy bed at night.

Take Time To Notice:

*How people are always trying to make things look pretty -----
their cars, lawns, homes, pets, hair, faces, etc.*

*How certain people you meet are just your kind of people right
after only a few words.*

*How intelligent children are these days. They use words at age
6 that I wasn't familiar with until age 16.*

How wonderful it feels to really love someone.

*How many people send greeting cards for no particular
reason.*

*How, when you feel good about yourself, it's easier to be nice
to others.*

*How many elderly people today put on their sneakers and go
walking!*

Take Time To Notice:

How many people are up bright and early hustling to keep the world turning.

How many people listen to and read self-help, self-improvement books.

How people still love gift giving.

How people with hot tempers soften after you listen to them and agree with them.

How you can make new friends anywhere if you go there day after day.

How, in spite of the high divorce rate, people are still getting married in hopes of living happily ever after.

How having a friend 30 years older than you is a priceless addition to your life.

Take Time To Notice:

How, if you look hard enough, you can find a greeting card to say exactly what you're thinking.

And really listen when someone offers advice. At least consider it sincerely before you decide to discard it.

How most of us can just get up and walk outside if we so choose.

How we all have precious memories forever sealed within ourselves, and no one nor anything can ever take them from us.

How negativity does breed negativity, yet goodness breeds goodness and the kind of friend you are is most likely the kind of friend you will attract.

How people will say about a wealthy person, "He has done real well for himself." All this means is that person is making a lot of money. We must stop and notice how people have done well

Take Time To Notice:

for themselves in mind, body, and spirit, compassion, understanding, and self appreciation.

How the more worth you put into your life, the more worthwhile it becomes.

How, even though our world is now motivated by the "High-Tech" locomotive, we still yearn for simplicity. We choose to take up as hobbies what our ancestors needed for survival--- fishing, hunting, gardening, walking, and sewing to name a few.

How people, who are surrounded by others all day in the business hustle bustle, find a few moments of quiet to be so very intoxicating.

How the people who really want to get things done...do!

Your relationships: no one likes rejection. Why is it okay to cast someone away, but we don't like them to walk away?

How every manmade object around you was someone else's job!

Take Time To Notice:

How, when you're not quite sure how you want to react to a certain situation, just being nice is always a good option. You won't regret what you've said, and it also buys you some time to process things and then handle them accordingly. How about instead of "Just say no" make your slogan "Just be nice!"

How hearing those familiar Christmas songs gives you that bitter-sweet sensation over and over again each season.

How encouraging it is to see so many people still eager to decorate for the holidays.

How, once we really get acquainted with ourselves we begin to recognize our faults, only then can we resculpt our personas and become better people. You have to intimately know yourself before you're capable of changing into that someone you admire.

Take Time To Notice:

How we busybodies actually feel guilty when we rest. We must stop to realize the entire world around us has an on and off pattern. The great ocean waves peak and ebb. Our major organs have this rhythm. Our lungs rest between exhaling and inhaling, just as our hearts rest after each life-sustaining beat.

How life only makes sense looking backwards, but we still must live it forwards.

How most all problems of the world, both big and small, both foreign and domestic, can still be solved by the ancient remedy called communication.

How everyone loves to be remembered. Make a concentrated effort to remember people's names, for these are still everyone's favorite words.

How, when you sit and watch the time pass by on the clock, those are seconds and minutes going by one at a time which you can never get back.

64

Take Time To Notice:

How the basic principles and needs still exist even in violence. All the cults and gangs call themselves family and brothers. They all still need to feel like a part of something, like someone needs them and they belong.

How some things never go out of style, such as grandma's adages. For example, "Two wrongs don't make a right...Haste makes waste, and don't throw stones if you live in a glass house."

How if you love doing a particular something, you will automatically become good at it.

How so many of us are identified by our careers. This goes all the way back to Biblical days. The disciples were identified first as... a tax collector, a fisherman, etc. Make the best of your lot in life. We can do so much good for others with each day. As Ecclesiastes 3:22 says: "There is nothing better for men than that they should be happy in their work, for that is why we are here."

Take Time To Notice:

How time is a much more valuable commodity than is money. There is always more money to be had if you want to work harder and gain more. But time is very precious. We cannot earn more even on good merit. We cannot speed it up nor slow it down. All we can do is spend it wisely and be fulfilled with its rewards. Some people say, "Time is money." I say, "Time is priceless."

What you are doing when you find you are most happy and content; then strive to do more of it.

How forgiveness is sometimes difficult, but most times easier than harboring the ill feelings that fester from the one who wronged you. Remember, it may not be easy to bend, but bending is better than breaking.

How it is impossible to keep new things new! Yet we try as with clothes, cars, homes, etc. Let us not overlook love. It also requires repair, maintenance and replenishment.

Take Time To Notice:

How even though we have so many forms of communication today, we still appreciate the opportunity to put a real voice and a face to a name.

That if you keep your face towards the sunshine, you won't see the shadows.

Worry! Even though I believe worrying is incurable, telling someone "Not to worry" always lends some element of relief. Worriers are plagued because worry is compounded with guilt and regret. I have many times actually worried myself sick. But I have two remedies that have helped to ease the pain: As my mother has told me:
"Worrying is like a rocking chair. It gives you something to do, but gets you nowhere." And Philippians 4:6:
Don't worry about anything: instead, pray about everything: tell God your needs and don't forget to thank Him for His answers. If you do this, you will experience God's peace which is far more wonderful than the human mind can understand, His peace will keep your thoughts and your hearts quiet and at rest as you trust in Christ Jesus.

Take Time To Notice:

That we are able to communicate with just about anyone if we truly want to. Some reactions denote a universal language regardless of nationality, age or handicap. Even deaf mutes display smiles and tears which have the same interpretation as yours. It's ok to reach out to everyone!

That you are the master of your own destiny because:
> *What you want out of life becomes what you think about all day*
> *What you think becomes what you say*
> *What you say becomes what you do*
> *What you do becomes habit*
> *Habits mold your character*
> *Your character outlines your destiny*

How love truly can make the world go around.

How every long, hard journey begins somewhere with just one step.

Take Time To Notice:

How things always seem to function better after some grooming and prep work. Our cars seem to run better once they are washed and shining. Isn't it funny, do you think it is just a coincidence that when you pay attention to your appearance you, too, function better when you look your best?

How you can parallel becoming a healthy Christian with bodybuilding. Start out gradually, lifting, strengthening, and becoming dedicated. Then you begin feeling better about your progress and you see results. Continue putting positive, nutritional things into your body, which creates a healthier outlook. Learn more and more about your passion, spread the word, read all you can, and associate with people who share your common interest and learn from their mistakes.

There are only a few things that can never be taken from you. Your studies and your travels are some that come to mind. Learn all you can and see all you can.

Take Time To Notice:

We all have a daily gift of being able to experience an all new 24 hours each day. We are all given the same 60 minutes in each hour and 60 seconds in each minute. Don't let a bad mood rob you of any episode in life. There are so many wonderful people you haven't yet met.

How it feels so refreshing and invigorating to slip into some nice new clothes. Try slipping into a nice new attitude each morning. It will feel wonderful! Even if it doesn't stay crisp all day, even if someone tears at your new attitude or dumps something on it, that's okay...because you're allowed to slip into a brand new one again tomorrow.

How we all complement each other in life. Just take a look around no matter where you are right now. Some genius made that television your watching and the couch that feels so cozy. Then go ahead, snuggle up with that enchanting story perfectly written, printed, and bound into a nice little book. It took several people just like you to manufacture that

tiny little cell phone to help you keep in touch. Someone else made your favorite wine to enjoy over the meal grown, harvested, and then prepared at your favorite restaurant. Yes, all this was done by little earthlings very much like you. Do all this while sporting that beautiful suit, tailored and sewn by yet someone else. Then maybe, what say, we take in a movie which was produced, directed, and acted out over long, hard hours by none other than some of your neighbors. Don't stop there. Hop into your perfectly engineered car designed by other fellow citizens. It will take you about anywhere you need to go if you keep it full of the fuel your gas station has pumped in for you to purchase. Need I continue? How could we ever dislike our peers? We are all in this together.

How handy a trash can is. At home I throw all my undesirables into it. I also have a personal trash can. I carry it with me and when I have an ill thought about someone or something, I try my best to throw them away in my portable trash can.

Take Time To Notice:

There is so much talk these days about investing in our futures: 401 K's, IRA's, Keough's and profit sharing. We must remember, however, to invest in our real futures, you know, the ones for eternity? We are all here only temporarily. Our eternal lives cannot be purchased with dollars, only with sense!

How it is impossible to preserve our outer bodies as we age. We see and feel yearly deterioration of our flesh and bones. We have little control over this decline. Isn't it nice to know that we have full control over our inner bodies and emotions? We can feed and provide our minds and spirits with all the right nutrients so they can grow ever stronger and healthier.

All the little things today because tomorrow, looking back, they will be the big things.

How we get so annoyed by all the interruptions when we're just trying to do our work! Maybe all those interruptions are our work...

Take Time To Notice:

How most traits are only ours temporarily--our beauty, nice figures and long lustrous hair are all impossible to hold on to. There are only a handful of things that we can preserve forever. Time cannot steal our sense of humor; we can laugh no matter what. Our love of nature can be kept even if we lose our sight; we have four other senses to enjoy it. And our love for God can never be stolen; we can only forfeit it or allow it to dwindle.

How everyone has fears, phobias, hang-ups, etc. It's so much better when we can recognize and admit them. Nothing can be trashed if it is hidden.

How rewarding it is to live every moment today as you would have loved to live yesterday.

How every minute you spend being angry is one less minute of happiness for you.

Take Time To Notice:

How when you become angry, many times if you dig deeply inside you'll discover that you're really not upset about what you think you are. If you are totally honest with yourself, you'll admit that many times you're actually disappointed with yourself about some inadequacy.

How you will earn a lot of admiration and trust if you are a good "secret keeper."

How even though our major cities are overcome with such gross squalor, the popular consensus want things to be clean! We are always trying to develop better cleaning techniques. A shinier car, more of a dust free home, a pollution controlled atmosphere, better detergents, etc. Isn't that nice?

How we can only detect a silver lining if it envelopes a dark, contrasting mass. We would not be able to discern happiness from despair if all our days were filled with bright, shining, illuminous substance. That is why we need a contrast in our

everyday world to have a full life.

How most fads go full circle. I hope that holds true for lifestyles; whereas one day we neighbors will come back to drinking homemade lemonade on one another's front porch.

How it is never too late to be a better person.

**When our mother had her disabling brain hemorrhage,
these are the things my family and I had to offer her.**

We gave her understanding as she learned to speak.

We gave her encouragement as she learned to walk.

We gave her patience as she learned to feed herself.

We gave her self-esteem when people looked at her oddly.

We gave her our time when she needed someone right next to her.

We gave her laughter to get through the incidentals.

We gave her pure love when we were unsure where to turn next.

And we gave her prayer to keep all our other gifts going.

Take Time To Notice: These are all free gifts.

Special Credits;

To my father, Delbert, who fell in love with his wife all over again. Remember, the best thing a father can do for his children is to love their mother.

To my sister, Janie, who shared my courage and focus all in the name of love for a common goal. Thanks for picking me up when I'd fall. I love ya!

To my sweet cousin, Audrey. Thank you for being one of my most loyal and supportive fans. Thank you for all your long hours of reading, rereading, editing, emending, and proofing. Thank you for so eagerly finding time for me that you really didn't have. You are one in a million and I am proud to call you "Cuz."

To all the many readers and promoters of my first book who have, by their encouraging words, made me a very wealthy person.

The Silver Lining

The Silver Lining

Part a: After Birth
Part b: Human Interest and Investment
Part c: Full Circle
Part d: God's Grace

Introduction to The Silver Lining

Silver linings in my life:

Strengthening from pain.

Learning how to sacrifice with ease.

Grasping for all of God's cues.

Attaining wisdom, growing from wisdom, and passing wisdom on to others.

Counting every day as a blessing, for tomorrow is promised to no one.

Looking at beauty beneath the surface.

Never discount that people can truly change for the better.

Finding that the right people are there when you need them if you are the right people for others.

God provides for you in all ways if you trust.

The most trivial moments hold the most value.

The Bible can tell you how to best handle any situation.

Grieving is a journey you have to go through, you can't avoid it, but you can survive it.

Live for today, dream for tomorrow, learn from yesterday.

Mother, Miss Carol Smith, upon graduation from Presbyterian Nursing School 1951.

Mummy circa 1960. She was often called upon to model for local clothing stores even after having four children.

Mummy at a wedding in 1976 with from left to right, son Mark, daughter Janie, herself, me at the far right and Janie's daughter, Kimberly, at the bottom.

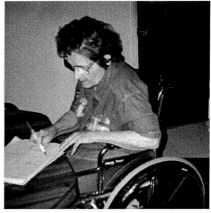

Mummy at the kitchen table in 1999. This was during one of her evening assignments when she was learning how to write all over again. Keep in mind, her right arm had been paralyzed and tightly retracted next to her body for a long time following her brain incident.

Mummy with her adored physical therapist, Craig, in the front yard in the spring of 2000. He was so very dedicated to her recovery and almost had her walking independently.

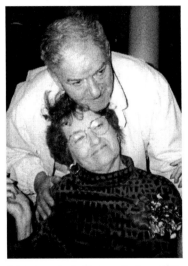

Mummy and Pappy at her 69th birthday. She was so extremely happy this day. October 14, 2000

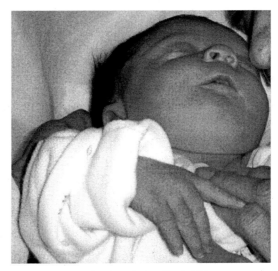

Mummy completing her circle. She held her new great granddaughter, Hannah Jane, on April 14, 2002, at 2:30. This was the first stop Hannah made after being discharged from the hospital. Mummy, though comatose, got a tear in her eye while holding her first great grandchild. Knowing her life was complete, Mummy left to be with her Maker 12 hours later. She just needed to touch Hannah and bless her with the gift of life.

After Birth

This segment of the book had to wait until after my mother's passing to take form. The beginning section was the outcome of how taking care of my mother opened my eyes wide enough to "Take Time To Notice." With that blessing of noticing, I now am abundantly rewarded with silver linings emotionally, physically, and spiritually. In my mother's desperate, totally dependent state, she unknowingly gave me an after birth. I am a completely different person than I was five years ago when she first became ill. I never knew while I was feverishly trying to heal my mother that I was actually mending my soul. She forced me to come full circle without even a suggestion. I stepped out of my children's shoes right into those of a parent's. I kept reminding myself that since I never had children this was my turn to sacrifice and give my all. I developed keen mothering techniques as I journeyed along. She pulled her share of pranks, such as hiding her pills underneath her tongue, then spitting them out when no one was looking. Some days she just would not do her therapy; many nights she would not sleep; some days she refused to get out of bed. At times she'd throw most of her meal on the floor for the dog! But you see, after investing so much of my human interest into her new life, I earned a new one of my own. I allowed my mother's circumstances to stretch me and push me to the limit. Now I'm

aware of my capabilities. It is one of the most gratifying feelings in the world to know I can make a difference. Now I know I can find that extra time to give to someone else.

God has made me aware of every moment of every day to enjoy, to reflect, to rest, to ponder, to grieve, instead of a scattered mix of nothing.

Becoming a Godly person happens overnight for some people. Then for some of us it is a gradual, growing, learning process. I spent many years asking myself; "Am I a Godly person yet? Have I proven myself to be a Christian yet"? There were times I actually felt guilty being so dedicated to my dental career. I thought that maybe I was allowing God to take a back seat in my travels. But, then again His handy guidebook, known better as the Bible, read to me about me! Colossians 3:23, " Work hard and cheerfully at all you do, just as though you were working for the Lord, not for people."

Also, since I never felt I was becoming a good enough person fast enough all I could do was just keep chipping away at it. Similar to a sculptor, I learned not to let all the daily little imperfections ruin my future image. Colossians 3:10, "You are living a brand new life now that is continually learning more and more of what is right, and trying constantly to be more and more like Christ who created this life within you." It was then I realized I had been transformed into a new being.

Mine was the gradual, but steady type of rebirth. I unconsciously evaluated my every thought and reaction to any given situation, good or bad. I notice daily how the sun reflects off the trees, how blue the sky is and how the moon illuminates our backyard. It was true; it had happened! Once I allowed God into my life I was definitely not the same person as years gone by. He had shown me that rather than just living and assimilating, I now, as second nature, monitor my every response to life's experiences to at least tip the scales and gravitate toward God's way. Once you allow Him in, hold on tight because life has an all-new meaning. Building your relationship with God can be very slow and not always precise. First, you realize God is there and wants to be your friend. Then, you start learning more and more about Him. Then, the next thing you know, you're talking to Him. Believe it or not, He starts talking back! Then once you are secure with knowing He is your friend to keep, you quit trying to figure out the plan by asking: "Okay, God, now what do you want me to do"? You just say, "God whatever you put before me I'll try to do my best."

After Mother's passing, many people would say to me, "Well, she suffered so long." I know they were just trying to ease my pain, but I don't look at it that way at all. My Mom had more love and affection funneled toward her in that four and one half years than she would have ever had if she hadn't gotten sick. I feel so blessed that God gave me

such opportunity to relish each beautiful moment with her. That was bonus time we almost didn't have after her brain injury. She was content most of the time; she didn't have enough of a brain process to actually worry about all the things that used to plague her. We just realized every day couldn't be a good day. For example, I weigh only 108 pounds soaking wet and my mother was a tall, hippy woman with those big "Smith Legs" as she would call them. Fortunately, we fell only a couple of times when I was trying to transfer her. Once I cracked a few ribs, but broken ribs heal and when we'd wind up on the floor I'd say, "Mummy, what do we do when we fall?" She'd reply, "We get back up again." So I certainly don't view her respite/recovery interval as suffering. God gave us a wonderful opportunity to return back to her only a sliver of all the sacrificing she did for us. Without even knowing it, her illness gave birth to an all new person in me. I am totally different in all thoughts, actions, and reactions. If the tragedy had never happened, I might still be lost out there somewhere. I would have God as my Ultimate Being, but I may never have found Him to this extent where He is inside me and I know He'll never leave me. Just as 2 Corinthians 5: 17 taught me, "When someone becomes a Christian, he becomes a brand new person inside. He is not the same anymore. A new life has begun!"

After my mother left me a sweet friend of mine sent me a beautiful and profound verse. In it was a line that said, "When you hear a song or see a

bird I loved, please do not let the thought of me be sad…For I am loving you just as I always had. You were so good to me 'twas heaven here with you"!

This has been so magical to me. My mother loved birds and she loved music and I have many precious memories of enjoying both of these with her. When I hear music she loved for a split second, I do get sad, but I then reminisce back to a beautiful sunny day when I'd take her for a ride in my convertible with the roof down and her favorite music blasting! We'd go and pick up Janie and Kim and the carload of us looked quite peculiar, I'm sure, with Mummy in a funny hat and all of us dancing and singing while cruising all over town. I am so grateful that at these moments I took time to notice and I have them deeply imprinted in my mind and now I can smile… So, rejoice when you see something reminiscent of a loved one that you shared in it with them here on earth.

I would advise anyone who loses a loved one to take possession of a trivial article of clothing of theirs and wear it proudly. I have some of my mother's jewelry and her better clothing, but they don't mean nearly as much as the two pairs of socks I inherited. In my mother's life prior to her brain damage she was not the type of lady to wear tennis shoes and athletic socks. However, they became her everyday attire, post brain trauma, to do her rehabilitation workouts. Well, when I put on a pair of

her socks my feet tingle, my legs feel energized and my heart is light. I love them. I just don't want them to wear out! They give me a rebirth.

Going through my own storms in life has intensely fine-tuned my perception of others' lifestorms. I can almost feel their heartache which can come as abruptly as a bolt of lightning. There is chaos just one layer down. A while back John and I were eating dinner when we got the saddening news that friends of ours had been in a bad car accident. A young mother and her two lovely children were thrust from a red light stopping point by a fast moving vehicle. The mother was taken to one hospital and the son to another. Thankfully, the daughter seemed to be okay and the father was not in the car with them. Having gone through my own turmoil in the past, I almost felt guilty continuing to just sit there and finish dinner while their lives had suddenly turned inside out. I knew how they must be feeling, so defeated in the eye of a hurricane. My mind started churning, what could I possibly do for them? I turned to John and said, "Normally I go up to my personal sanctuary (my bedroom) and pray. That's what I need to do." John responded, "No, we'll pray together." At that very moment there was positively nothing else we could have done for them. Prayer is such a gift we can have any time to give to anyone. People can never have too many of them; they are free for the asking and they are always available.

Sit a while and let me relate a whimsical story to you about joy, tears and reward with an unusual musical slant...

This incident goes back to May 1998. My mom was recuperating at The Greenery facility. Spring had sprung and it was a most beautiful, crisp day. I had taken the day off from work and planned a full day of activities with her. When I arrived, she was sitting up in bed, very alert and said, "I've been waiting on you"! That menial welcome was so precious to me, as we never knew what to expect. Many days Mother was in a fog-like daze with no conception of time, place and / or company. I then read my daily note from Kristy, the occupational therapist. Kristy came to Mother's room early in the mornings, and she knew how closely we monitored progress. We had a system where she'd make notes of each day's early events. Kristy noted that Mummy woke up happy, talkative, and eager to help dress herself. Mummy gave me one of those big, enveloping hugs that always devoured me and then told me she loved me. What a relief from all the long days Janie and I put in with Mummy not speaking a word, having yet another malady and just lying in bed instead of going to therapy. Well, today was different! We had a busy schedule ahead! Off we went to speech therapy. Marsha, the speech therapist, was so very impressed. Mummy carried on a more lucid conversation than ever. She identified miscellaneous objects and told us when she needed to go to the bathroom. The next joy was physical therapy. Mummy was comical. She whispered to me that if she "didn't do the right thing she

was going to get hollered at." With that in mind, she walked down the hallway, leg brace intact, holding onto a shopping cart with only a little assistance from Rob, her feared therapist. What a glorious day to behold! Of course, I went to the pay phone and called both Dad and Janie to lift their spirits as well. I had to repeat every spoken word of hers verbatim because we all held on so dearly to anything Mummy verbalized. Could this be some miraculous breakthrough? It certainly was a miracle for that day. Maybe Mummy had finally achieved some kind of new plateau???

Then we went back to the room and both took a short nap. I wanted to take her out to the courtyard to absorb some sunshine, but first, this was pampering day. I'd brought a radio from home assuming I would need means of stimulating a lethargic patient. Not today! She was definitely the one stimulating me! I trimmed and polished her nails, plucked her eyebrows and was shaving her legs while Sonny and Cher bellowed out "I Got You Babe." One would normally relate that song to a romantic couple, right? Well. How appropriate its lyrics were that day to me and Mummy: "I got you to walk with me. I got you to talk with me. I got you to kiss goodnight. I got you to hold me tight. I got you, I won't let go. I got you to love me so." She sang, I sang, she laughed, I cried…tears of joy that is.

All we had to do yet was wash, trim and dry her hair. I wanted to wait until after our time outside for that. Mummy and I sat outside for almost an hour. She was so much more aware of her surroundings that afternoon.

She commented on the birds singing and even talked a little to another lady outside who was enjoying the day from her wheelchair. Then it was time to go back indoors and complete our grooming routine. I did a quick wash of her hair as best I could with her sitting in an upright position. I then proceeded to the challenge of trimming as her "hairdo" was still all askew. The many different hair lengths served as reminders of the numerous times her head had been shaven in preparation for all the brain surgeries. Also, at some sections of the scars, and where the titanium plate was inserted, the hair chose not to grow back so we needed to try and disguise those areas. Shortly after I commenced to blow- drying and styling her hair Mummy suddenly started to grimace and then the entire left side of her face was uncontrollably twitching. Then her left extremities started with tremors and she lost bladder control. I ran out into the hallway and screamed, "something is wrong with my mother"! Debbie, a large framed nurse, entered the room and very calmly said to me, "go and get help." The next thing I knew, there was a team of six hovering over Mummy. A respiratory therapist yelled, "she's not breathing"! Then one of the nurses blared, "get her daughter out of here"! Oh God, what could have possibly gone wrong literally in the blink of an eye? Our beautiful day had abruptly been severed. As I sat, crouched-down in the hallway, once again I questioned, is this it? Is my mummy going to die? Is this already the end to our glory days of recovery? By this time my sister had arrived and I hysterically told her of the critical

change. About 20 minutes later we learned that Mummy seemed to be coming around. She'd had the worst, and longest lasting, grand mal seizure they had ever witnessed. The nursing staff told us Mummy would be very drowsy for the rest of the day and most likely all of the following day. They would monitor her even more closely because many times these types of seizures occur back to back. Janie decided to stay there with her all night and within two hours our dear mother was fine. Not sleepy, sitting up in bed, talking well and bouncing to her music!!! So typical of Mummy. She never did follow the rules and did a good job of defying the medical books...

I thank God for allowing me to have in my "memory-bank" such colorful images of scenes as that day. I guess the moral to the story here is; embrace the gifts given us each day, know that we must give gifts in return, and no gift sparkles forever. This day, like so many others, made me realize I am always going to have times in my strife when I question: "God, what do You have going on here"? But I never doubt that He is there. It took me a very long time to stop begging God to hold on and not separate us from Mummy just yet. It took me an even longer time to quit pleading with Mummy to stay strong and not to leave us, not yet... It took me a whole lot of praying and soul-searching to come to the realization that I couldn't keep on trying to tell God what to do! He is very gracious and merciful but still the "Ultimate Physician," and He knows best. Another full circle, after birth revelation, which grew from

humanitarian aid and understanding God's plan of the "big picture."

Human Interest and Investment

While caring for my mother we'd occasionally fall. I mean literally fall to the ground. Fortunately, she never really got hurt during any of our escapades, but one day in particular comes to mind. As we struggled to get back up off the floor, I said, "Mummy, you know how life is when we fall, we just get back up." She responded, "and maybe with each fall, we'll get bruised less and less, huh"?

This is such an uplifting story about someone I barely knew at the time. John and I frequent a quaint, little Italian restaurant just a few miles from our home. The "Chef Extraordinaire" there is named Demetrius. Throughout the evenings at the restaurant he would visit with all the patrons just to make certain that everyone was pleased with his Italian creations. Since we were usually some of his latecomers after our workday, Demetrius normally had a little more free time to spend with us, so he'd pull up a chair to chat a spell. During our short, sporadic conversations Demetrius would always interject a statement or two regarding his five-year-old son, Cody. Demetrius was divorced and Cody lived with him so he was the one responsible for tending to all of his son's needs. On different

occasions Demetrius mentioned having Cody enrolled into kindergarten, taking him to doctors' appointments and doing whatever was necessary to be certain Cody had competent babysitters while he was at work. Demetrius' voice was so proud and compassionate with any comments concerning his wonderful son. I also noted what a tremendous work ethic he possessed along with great people skills. He made it clear that he didn't mind working so many long, hard days because Cody deserved a good life. I said to him one night, "Demetrius, how did you get such wisdom at only 31 years of age"? He replied, "Well, I've been through a lot"! It wasn't until that evening after numerous conversations about Cody that he revealed his son was born with only one eye, one kidney, and one thumb. He had already undergone 13 operations at the age of five. He explained that Cody was still deficient with all of these birth defects; the many surgeries were to improve his brain growth which was only nine percent developed at birth. None of Cody's shortcomings were ever mentioned before during our talks—only his qualities. After Demetrius told us all they had gone through as a father and son team, he said, "I'm going to bring him with me when I come down to your office. You'll get to meet him; he's a great kid"! All I could think was how fortunate Cody was that Demetrius was chosen to be his dad.

I have since met Cody. What a gift he truly is. He fills a room with love and is one of the most affectionate children I know. It's easy to see how all of his endowments camouflage any imperfections.

Remember, do the best with what is before us…

I will be very pleased to see the day when we have just one broadcasted television station delegated to only daily, random acts of kindness. I know there are enough of them going on out there to fill a day of viewing. Some people have over 100 different channels to skip through. Let's just have one that is non-fiction, easy to comprehend, no mysterious cliffhangers, and where everyone is the "Good Guy." Wouldn't it be nice to have your children sit down after school and listen to a five-year-old boy talking about his beach vacation and saying his favorite part was "Spending time with his family," or who shared their one candy bar with three other children? I'd love to see, on film, the way old folks light up when someone takes the time to visit with them or surprise them with a little birthday gift. There are many who voluntarily clean our highways and offer their services at animal shelters. Sure, there are still many cats and dogs without homes, but there are an abundance of them which are adopted. My cousin, for example, has given refuge to 13 cats at one time. Perhaps someone simply helped a tiny bird, not quite ready to fly, to get back in its nest. There are countless supporters who donate

vast amounts of money and time to charities all over the world and we don't hear nearly enough about them. The Guatemalean twins who were born conjoined at the head were separated in a California hospital in August 2002. The procedure was a 22-hour surgery and the attending neurosurgeons donated their time. I learned of a family somewhere in the Pittsburgh area who has taken in 11 disabled children who were destined to be homeless. Recently, Cost Cutters Hair Salons sponsored a charity drive. A free haircut was given to anyone with hair over 12 inches long. The snipped off remnants were to be donated to "Kids With Cancer." I am convinced that turning on one's television and being inundated with surges of beautiful humanitarian acts would have such a positive impact on society.

These books are my biggest silver lining. My mother's story and strength can live on forever. Many people ask me, "What really made you decide to write a book"? Well, other than it was a nice alternative to having a nervous breakdown, I believe it came mainly from a revelation and a rude awakening I had. During my mother's five month stay at the hospital [incidentally, she became known as "you know, that lady who's been here forever"] I spent many hours in the chapel. Since she became ill in November she was there right through the Thanksgiving and Christmas holidays. Well, so were we... During those visits to pray in the chapel I did indeed physically hurt;

my heart was so heavy it made me feel as though I was unable to sense anything other than sadness. It was then I realized how naïve I had been. I had just been coasting through life and never truly knew how many people out there had hurt like this and will hurt like this. At Christmas the chapel had a Christmas tree with hanging paper ornaments where you could write down what you most desired for your holiday gift. The heart rendering wishes from all the suffering hearts hanging on that tree made me realize that I wanted to do more. Now that I have my first book in circulation, it is so gratifying when someone tells me, "Joni, I just read something in your book and it gets me through the day," or " I just learned that so and so is really sick and I want to give him or her one of your books to lift their spirits." What more could I ask for? This is exactly what I intended the book to do, even if it helps only a handful of people. Remember, you can never help everyone, but you can always help someone...

Here are some creative, helpful ways to invest your human interest into caring for a loved one: I made audio tapes for my mother to listen to even as she recovered from a coma in the hospital. They were tapes with my voice to stimulate her brain regarding who she was, when and where she was born, who her parents and siblings were, everything from when her parents came from Austria to present day ages of her children and grandchildren. She was enchanted with

these tapes up until a few weeks before passing. I made flash cards for her with the days of the week, the months of the year, and numbers from one to ten. She learned to put them in the proper sequence on the table. She was never able to read again, but somehow, just from association, her long-term memory knew in what order they belonged. Then we also recorded both audio and video tapes of her favorite music. This would pacify her for hours. Then at times we would play games with her to identify smells. She usually wasn't able to come up with a response on her own, therefore, we would give her choices. For example, we'd have her close her eyes and smell vanilla, then ask her, "Is it vinegar, lemon or vanilla"? Most times she was able to come up with the correct answer. We also had a work-out room made for her in the basement, complete with parallel bars, bicycle pedals, an exercise bench and matt. We had a chair glide installed to get her up and down the steps of her make-shift gym. At times with her extensive brain damage she would get obsessive/compulsive with the issue of the day. Sometimes she demanded lots and lots of sugar. With her neurologic state, many days she wasn't able to focus on much of anything beside eating. She would forget that she had just eaten five minutes earlier and her brain kept registering to her that she was starving. Other days, she would insist that she couldn't see and wanted new glasses, even though she had just been to two eye doctors and had new glasses. Since she had

no short-term memory she was convinced some days that she was not clean and persisted until we washed her three and four times. This is by no means an easy task with a 5'6" woman who cannot stand on her own and wants to be assured she is clean from head to toe. Then there were those periods when she'd say she was nervous and needed a nerve pill. Well, we could bluff our way through for a while with harmless amounts of vitamins and herbs, but when she requested one every ten minutes even those could be abused. Finally, we came up with the idea of letting her have some control. We bought some Equal tablets, put them in a prescription bottle and left then on the stand next to where she sat in the living room. This remedy proved to be very advantageous to all involved. Since she was a retired nurse she felt some autonomy in knowing her proper dosage and could get one (or two or three) any time she felt like it. We didn't have to try and reason with her as to why she couldn't have a nerve pill five or six times in any given hour. Then there was the crash course I took in reflexology to massage and stimulate pressure points on her feet to encourage recovery in both her brain and her flaccid foot. I even bought some very expensive "brain gum" that was proven to promote regeneration of brain cells. I just didn't want to overlook any possibility that may benefit her.

Last, but not least, ever take time to notice how every crisis somehow turns into a financial issue? Well, it didn't take my dad long to go through their savings. Everyone was unanimous in agreeing that Mummy was worth every last cent. We children helped all we could and when that still wasn't enough, my brother, Mark, came up with an idea. We children bought their home. This way my father had that lump sum of money to live off, they weren't in danger of losing their house and my siblings and I split the monthly mortgage. You know, when someone closes a door, you-know-who always opens a window!!! It worked out splendidly. You'll have such peace in the end when you know you've done all you could.

Overall, people are so kind. I urge anyone to take time to notice this. For two years in a row when my mother was wheelchair-bound we took her to see a live concert with one of her all-time favorite groups, "The Platters." This band was more than altruistic with Mummy. The lead singer, Sonny Turner, dedicated a song to her, put the spotlight on her more than once and even incorporated her name into another song he sang. Needless to say, she was thrilled. The whole band was so kind to her. They gave her a pin and a personalized T-shirt. The second year Sonny recognized her with his button on and said, "Oh, there's my girl"! He then came over, allowed her to steal the show again, serenaded her and, of course, overwhelmed her.

These evenings, needless to say, were perfect ones. We were blessed, and all because someone else took time to notice my mother...

Here's a story, for your enjoyment, about one of my guardian angels. At the dental office where I work there is a lady across the street who owns our parking lot. Her name is Mrs. Krutz. Mrs. Krutz was used to seeing me getting in and out of my car for work with about the same schedule for well over 10 years. We'd exchange "good mornings" and many times she'd invite me in for coffee and a chat. Well, shortly after my mom became ill in November of 1997, Mrs. Krutz noticed my daily routine had been thrown way out of whack! I was coming and going at unusual times, not looking left nor right to see if my friend was around and was even more hasty than she normally saw me. Mrs. Krutz took it upon herself to look into the matter of my new erratic behavior. Our office informed her of my mother's misfortune and from that day on, almost every day for eight months, when I bolted out of the office to make my one hour commute to the hospital or rehab facility, I would find a care package dangling from the door handle of my car. I would find maybe a sandwich, fried chicken, cookies and or fruit in my portable" Krutzy-Style" lunch bag. Well, I was always burning rubber to get to my mother's side quickly as we tried not to leave her alone for any length of time. My sister and I worked out a coordinated schedule so that she

would leave at a designated time and I would arrive shortly afterwards. Whatever dear Mrs. Krutz hung on my car that day was exactly what I would have for my dinner. Even though the state of mind I was in at that time left me with no appetite, my daily transportable meals surely did taste good and otherwise I would have most likely eaten nothing. Thank you Mrs. Krutz for taking time to notice…

It is so astounding how adaptable we really are. When my mother first became critically ill, I had been working at the dental office for over 13 years. During that 13 years I had never once called off sick, left early, or slept in and arrived late. I was already super-stretched out with time and usually worked about 55-60 hours a week. As you can imagine, the bottom certainly fell out when my efforts were suddenly needed elsewhere. It was compulsory that I miss work some days to be with my mother, and when I was at work my day was incessantly interrupted with phone calls regarding my mother. What a drastic change for me, Dr. John, and the other girls. When mother was at home I would sleep with her at night. We usually had paid help for only an eight-hour-shift during the day. That meant that my 10-12 hour days at the office were out of the question. Also, since I had to wait for a caregiver in the morning and had to relieve her at night that meant I came in later every morning on the job and needed

to leave early every evening. Our patient schedule was somewhat restructured. I couldn't rely on everyone else to do all of my work. No more surgical procedures could be scheduled first thing in the morning (as was protocol) since you-know-who was going to be late. Everyone was so flexible, however, with changing our routine. All those years I was just positive that the office could not operate without me. I knew for a fact that I had to be the first one there in the morning and the last employee to leave at the end of the day. Well, surprise! People are so resilient, life is so resilient and we all just make it work! I am now working more regular hours ... the office survived! The building didn't burn down; we still have lots of wonderful patients, and we manage to pay the bills. I invested my human interest into my most important commodity for four and one-half years and life was still there waiting for me in the end.

Full Circle

Taking care of my mother for four and one-half years was, at times, all-consuming and I would wonder: How long can my family and I endure this? How long will the money last? What if something happens to my sister or me?...Always uncertainty. We even tried the route of admitting her into a personal care home. This decision came about after several coincidental mishaps. I ended up in the hospital emergency room with a presumed stomach ulcer, my father had just been diagnosed with artery blockages in both legs and was scheduled for surgery and my sister had pneumonia. So Janie and I sought what we believed to be the best personal care home in our area. Mother was taken in as a resident, but this stay lasted only two and one-half months. After we all recuperated and regrouped, we took her back home. The silver lining here is that taking care of our mother proved to be the best thing any of us could have ever done with our lives even when we stumbled and missed a few steps. She had someone with her for that four and one-half years every second of every minute of every day. God was always showing me how to step out of the shadows. He talked to me so much through my Mother. Yes, through my mother who had her speech center destroyed, and if she ever spoke again she would have only a very limited vocabulary; that is according to the

neurosurgeons. Mummy would be the most "with it" when we would settle into bed for the night. We would lie there and reminisce about anything and everything. More than once she told me, "Honey, I want you to promise me that when the Good Lord comes for me, you won't worry. I've made my peace with God and I'll be ready." She also told me once that she wanted to enjoy her family all she could because she'd live to be only 70. This proved to be true.

God has given me so much personal wealth through allowing our mother to become totally dependent on her family. What at first seemed like a plague turned into a blessing. Because of this I feel her presence with me always. Sure, I do grieve at times, but I know she is with her Creator, and He can take better care of her than anyone.

If you've ever seen someone critically ill you'd know how distorted and unnatural they can look. During one of the episodes when my mother was on deaths door, her ICU Dr. told us, "I can't imagine someone being sicker than your mother is right now." She was so swollen that even the whites of her eyes were expanded and her eyelids were turned inside out. Then she had blood clots in her leg and, therefore, no circulation to her foot. I had always assumed that with lack of adequate blood flow perhaps the extremities would turn a bluish color. Well, much to my horror that day, when I picked up the sheet a BLACK foot was unveiled. Unbelievable to my eyes. The

silver lining to this? How wondrous our bodies are. These unfathomable set backs can actually be overcome and reversed. How can such a discolored body part go from black, almost necrotic tissue to a healthy pink flesh color again? Our human temples are such fascinating machines with unexplained capabilities. They can come full circle time and time again.

Think for a minute and equate your complexion with the sky. Imagine the rain as your tears. At this time of storm your face is dark and cloudy. No one really rallies around you when you're just one continuous downstream. However, if it is short-lived this purging does bring new life and allows you to regroup and return to everyday life. But a steady downpour of week-long rain can cause monumental problems with flooding and draining of your life and, perhaps, all you've worked for.

Then think of the beautiful, clear, blue sky as your bright, cheery complexion. A few cloudy blemishes usually go unnoticed, as long as you glow and beam right through them. The whole world wants to share your joy when you are sunny. You can bring them up with a single smile and help all those around to flourish. When you are not quite as bright maybe you have something bothering you. Then you are kind of overcast and just need to saunter through the day with the breeze, back and forth until you have jostled the problem around

enough to find a solution. Don't blow in the wind too long and get lost, just enough to sway towards a direction. A few showers here and there are very rejuvenating to find what is real and encourage new growth as long as you don't become drenched with the soggy burden that will weigh you down.

Would you prefer to be around someone who shines, incites energy and helps you to be productive all day or someone who is dark and dismal? There's not much to do on a dreary, rainy day. Notice most people stay indoors to themselves. Bad weather, just like a bad outlook, limits what one can do throughout the day. Many activities, which could have taken place to add joy to your life, are cancelled or postponed to a nicer day. Don't put your life on hold for a better day. Come full circle and do what you have to do today.

Coming full circle in life to me means to experience every kind of weather, then having the wisdom to sift through your many seeds and sow the most superior ones. Let them get rooted in the very best soil. Make sure you nurture them to build a strong foundation. Don't allow them to weaken by being exposed to deteriorating creatures, and disinfect as soon as possible if there is any contamination. If you follow these simple steps you are guaranteed to yield premium results!

Another angel at work…there is a girl who worked at the post office in the small town where I work. Her name is Kathy Greenwood. Every year in late spring or early summer Kathy would give me a caterpillar that was destined to transform into a beautiful monarch butterfly. I don't believe Kathy realizes to this day what those gifts meant to me. The first year she gave me one was when my mom was in the rehabilitation center. I took the metamorphosing larva with me everywhere so as not to miss any dramatic changes and since my mother loved nature, it was a good focal point of fascination for her. Somehow, watching the life cycle of that little creature gave me comfort. It kind of mimicked the transformation my mother was going through at that time. Even though I knew monarch butterflies do not live long, I felt confident that my mom was going to experience a series of beautiful changes that would enable her to sprout a pair of wings and soar for a while in a brand new life with us.

My mother's parents, Frank and Camille, both came to the United States from Austria. Grandpap Frank (better known to us children as "Grandpap out the farm") was very close to being a saint! He was the purest of the pure—one of the most pleasant, hard working, honest individuals imaginable. His family came to this country in 1900 on a steamship voyage of 15 days. Their family came across the great

oceans with a meager $24 in their pockets and just an abundance of faith in their hearts. His parents raised 12 children in all and even in the early 1900's believed education was of utmost importance. Of my 12 great aunts and uncles there were two ministers, three school-teachers, three nurses and I believe a couple who entered trade schools-electricians, carpenters, etc. As an adult my grandfather worked full time in the steel mill, tended to a huge farm, delivered milk early in the mornings, and all the while was perpetually buying and remodeling old, dilapidated houses. He lived this kind of daily schedule and still found time to read his Bible everyday and attend church services each Sunday. Talk about being stressed? He was still an excellent husband and father to four children and spoke not a bad word about anyone. Can you imagine, he did all this without a drinking or drug problem? He didn't just put in his time waiting to earn a reward of a beach vacation or a Caribbean cruise. I keep hoping since history repeats itself, perhaps living life this way will come full circle. No harm in thinking positive, right?

Grandma Camille was a very staunch, strict person. She was so very refined. She came from Austria as a young teenager and as soon as she was settled in the U.S. one of the first things on her agenda was attending a finishing school. She didn't want to sound like a foreigner, so she studied and quickly grasped the English language

which she spoke grammatically correctly and carried no German accent whatsoever. She was almost a woman ahead of her day and was so devout and strict that she didn't even allow so much as a deck of playing cards in the house. Definitely no alcohol either and she never, I mean never, sat around the home in a robe and slippers. She always wore a dress, stockings and high-heeled shoes. She wasn't the kind of cuddly grandmother you would climb up into her lap to nestle with, but always set forth a good example of high standards and ethical values. My grandparents did amass very adequate wealth, but all from good, old, hard work. Here are some favorite words of wisdom from "Grandpap out the farm":

"All I every really want is a nickel more than I need."
"When you feel sick, the best thing for you is to go to work. It'll take your mind off of it."
"Why should I ask someone else to do something for me when I am quite capable of doing it myself?"

Grandpa Frank definitely had high standards for himself, but expected very little from anyone else. I am so blessed to have this kind of background in my family. I pray that as our world evolves through generations, life comes full circle and passes on these old world attributes.

It is a beautiful experience when you have daily reminders of God being in your life. Once you let Him in, He will never leave your side. Sure things will still go wrong, but you'll know how to handle and accept them so much more easily. Five years ago I was constantly anxiety-ridden about my mother's condition. She was sleeping too much, then not sleeping enough, eating too much then not eating enough, having too many bowel movements, then not enough!!! I continually found something to worry about, but God always pointed me in the right direction to overcome. After spending so much quality time with my mom I am so at peace with her passing. We had to give her back to God in His own time. For some unknown reason in November of 2001, she slipped into a coma. She had no fluids nor nourishment for six or seven days. As a family we were all adamant with, " no more surgery" and, again, planned her funeral. Then in true "Carol fashion," she miraculously regained consciousness and said she was hungry! I now believe she was waiting to sacrifice her life for her first great granddaughter's life whose due date into this world was the exact day Mother decided to really leave us. Hannah Jane arrived three days ahead of schedule and was born at 2:30 on April 12, 2002. My mother held her at 2:30 on April 14, 2002. Then Mother left us to be with God at 2:30 on April 15, 2002....

Coming full circle is such an adventure. You normally don't end up at your desired destination, but it still takes you to a satisfying end after a complete journey, which has exhausted all avenues. Ultimately, you're in a better place nonetheless. My brother has had a chronic drug addiction for almost 30 years. He first started with using marijuana when he was in the army and over the years has graduated to intravenous use of heroin. He has run the whole gamut of smoking joints to lots of pills, then on to cocaine and now his present end-of-the-road dependency on heroin. This is the same sibling who was very responsible when he was an adolescent. He worked many jobs by his own motivation just to buy himself nice cars and the latest in fashionable clothing. He was voted the best dressed in his high school graduating class, and could have anyone he chose to call his girlfriend. To see him today you would not know he was that same person. He has no car, no home, not even so much as a credit card or checking account, and owns only a few shabby clothes to work in. His three children call him by his first name and, for the most part, were raised by their stepfathers. It is truly sad that drugs are stronger than any relationship. My brother has had four women in his life who have honestly and sincerely loved him. We always teased Mummy that he was her favorite because of all her deep concerns for him. His children are loving and respectful and try to live life by the rules. One is a flight attendant, one an insurance agent and, his youngest is only

eight years old. To this day my brother earns $25- $30.00 per hour on the job, when he works. What is wrong with this picture??? All I know is when he was in his twenties, I assumed "well surely he'll get over this craze by the time he's thirty." Then at thirty, I was certain he wouldn't be able to keep up that lifestyle when he was forty. In his forties, I just knew he would follow the path of all his druggie buddies and reform with them since he was running out of friends. Well, here he is fifty and, guess what? Even seeing his beloved mother struggling for her life five years ago wasn't enough. He was devastated when he first saw her directly following the brain surgery. I remember he fell to the floor in the ICU and cried to God, "Please take me instead of her," and I know he meant it. On the way home that day I pleaded with him, "Please get clean for Mummy. When she recovers she will be so relieved and proud of you." He still couldn't do it, not even for the one person in his life he truly loved. The silver lining here is not that my brother came full circle to defeat his drug problem, but that I did in dealing with his dependency. Early on with the realization of his addiction, I had high hopes of saving him. I was instrumental with helping him get admitted into rehab facilities, learning all I could about the demons of his illness, paying his bills, sending letters of encouragement and just letting him know I was there for his children or whatever he needed. Well, you see, then I ran the gamut. I tried everything I knew from being supportive and

understanding, to lecturing and trying to reason with him. Then, for a time I just ignored the problem as though it didn't exist. I'd go from begging, to getting bitter then, just looking the other direction. I've prayed, prayed, prayed and asked my brother to pray for himself as well. But, now I have finally realized, I am no where near as strong as that drug that has abducted him and stolen his heart. No one can compete. He is the only one who can plot and pull off the great escape. These unrelenting, powerful forces have my brother and, he has left behind a family who loves him very much. He believes I no longer care about him simply because I refuse to give him money to aid in his addiction. It has taken me decades to conclude that only when he helps himself can anyone else be of help. For a while I even stopped praying for him. Now I only ask that if it is in "His" will, may God show my brother how to surround himself with the right people who could lead him to our one and only Savior. What else is left? I have completed my circle, but his is still just an open ended arc with a gap only he can close by allowing God to intervene.

My intention is not to imply, in any way, that I'd condone disowning a family member. I forgive my brother for everything. Just as Jesus states in Matthew: 18, verse: 21 when asked by Peter: " Shall I forgive my Brother as many as seven times"? Jesus replies: "You shall forgive him seven times seventy times." In other words, forgive him always.

Forgiveness does not mean allowing the needy person to lower you to their standards. Forgiveness, to me, means once they ask your forgiveness and you grant it, it translates into not holding a grudge, not reliving the circumstances, and no reminders of their shortcomings. Exonerate the wrongdoer totally and start fresh from that moment. I would be the first in line to assist in a recovery if my brother sincerely did create a change. I am onto his "pretend changing antics." I now know what to look for to ensure a true reformation. The following is a list of recovery signs that will occur in a genuine rehabilitation. I am told that, most times, all of them will take place simultaneously.

1. The recovering addict will start helping others with their same disease.
2. He or she will begin taking better care of their appearance.
3. He or she will want to work as much as possible at their jobs.
4. They will start to do volunteer work.
5. They will make amends with loved ones whom they have hurt in the past, and, they will not ask them for any more favors.
6. They will surround themselves with good people.
7. They will start going to church to make peace with God

If someone earnestly wants a new life he is free to merely go and get one.

It is quite true with every dark cloud there is a silver lining. It's been over five years since my mother's illness began. She had made tremendous progress through those recovering years. At her peak she was getting daily therapy, walking up and down our front steps with help, playing Chinese checkers and Old Maids with us. She became very conscientious and disciplined about her personal hygiene and bathroom habits. She would look forward to going to church, concerts, family functions or just for a ride in the car. We even had a birthday party for her when she turned 69 with over 60 of her close friends and relatives present. At this time she took the microphone and thanked everyone for coming. At Christmastime we would go shopping and she was capable of picking out the pair of pajamas she wanted to buy for Pappy and then she'd count out her own money to pay for them. Granted, with the amount of brain damage she sustained, there were many days when she was not herself, to say the least. On a bad day my family and I referred to her as "Reagan" because she rather mimicked that character from "The Exorcist." She would use profane language toward all of us closest to her and be quite unmanageable overall. We would give each other a "heads-up" and say; "Reagan's here today!" However, those bad days just made us really cherish all the beautiful days. The next day she would be totally unaware of yesterday's fiascoes. The entire family soon learned that caring for someone with part of their brain surgically

removed is a very unpredictable and an intensely humbling, patience-provoking experience. But the good days were the silver linings, when she'd listen to her favorite doo wop music and dance in her chair or help with dinner and the dishes. She wasn't quite aware of all the medical mishaps she had endured and she'd say, "Honey, I love you and God is so good to me."

When my great niece was born, my mother was terminally ill. What a play on emotions that day! I was back and forth from the hospital delivery room, filled with delightful anticipation, then, checking in with Mummy during her last days on earth, filled with dismal anticipation. During one of my jaunts from my mother to the hospital I tried to parallel the two situations. It dawned on me...if little Hannah has anything that resembles a thought process just yet, I'm sure she is so afraid. She is about to leave the safe, warm, comfortable womb of her mother to be part of a new, unforeseen life. How frightening it must be to leave the security of her nine-month residence to venture out into the unknown. But, then I realized what a glorious surprise to Hannah when she enters her new life and finds such a loving welcome in the arms of her earthly mother and father. Soon she will know that she is blessedly safe. Well, the same turn of events was in store for Mummy. She was about to leave her earthly home, but would be met with even a more magnificent reception by

her Heavenly Father. I thought of my mother just lying there in bed. She was so peaceful. She wasn't afraid, so I shouldn't be either.

A silver lining?… My mother died at age 70 with so few gray hairs that they could be plucked out and within seconds she'd have none. The body is so resilient if we treat it right. In the hospital it seemed that just as soon as her hair would start to grow back, they would shave it again for some surgical procedure. But amazingly so, it seemed each time it grew back in healthier than the time before.

My mother was transferred to the rehab facility, The Greenery, after five long months of medical uncertainty. We knew for sure she had very little short-term memory and we were still trying to get a grasp on how much long-term memory she retained. We never wanted to accept the devastating possibility that she may never remember her family or any of the past we shared. At The Greenery they offered a wide range of therapies. Along with the typical speech, occupation, and physical therapy programs, they also extended to their patients recreational and, my favorite, music therapies. I was overwhelmed with this. How wonderful for people to get their heads together and come up with such a motivating curriculum. Well, since my Mom was a music lover I figured this would be the true test. At her first session the music therapist played a guitar and sang "You Are My

Sunshine." Well, don't you know, my mother reached over, grabbed my hand, chimed right in and sang the entire second verse with no prompting. We all then sang together... "You are my sunshine, my only sunshine, you make me happy when skies are gray. You'll never know dear how much I love you, please don't take my sunshine away." What a happy day! Hence, the theme for my books.

God's Grace

One night when I was about nine years old my Mom, for some reason, said she would sleep with me. Perhaps my Dad was away hunting, but I remember my sister, who usually shared my bed, was across the street staying with her friend for the night. I was in the midst of saying my prayers and, after my customary dedication, I said to God, "Dear Lord, thank you that my mother hasn't taken any of her spells lately." [When my mother would have epileptic seizures they would form a pattern. The debilitating condition would last approximately five days and the seizures would happen a couple of times daily at which time she would pretty much stay in bed. We kids would refer to this as "Mummy's taking spells."] Just a few minutes into my prayer Mummy left out a very shrieky scream and went into one of her "spells." At first I thought she was yawning or starting to laugh, but when I turned on the light.....I knew..... That familiar, horrible, sick, weakening feeling coursed through my body. I ran down two flights of steps to the basement where my brothers' bedroom was. Then right before I proceeded to awaken them, I stopped and realized there was nothing they could do and it was my duty to care for my mother. I turned and went back upstairs to her. She had almost come out of the

seizure and had wet the bed. I just laid with her and prayed even harder. By morning she realized what had happened. She was always so ashamed of her epilepsy that she wouldn't even admit it to most people. Throughout my childhood this condition was always such a fearful threat hanging over my head that I recall always counting the months, sometimes a year in between occurrences and being so grateful for that reprieve but yet always knowing that it was undoubtedly going to strike again. As a child I was ill and hospitalized often. When I was five years old I contracted hepatitis, at six, I had a very serious case of the mumps. Then, at seven years of age, I lost my footing while playing in the church yard and fell backwards over a concrete ledge and down to the bottom of a full flight of block steps. I sustained a double fractured skull and the doctors told my parents I may not survive through the night. More of God's grace here is that mother was never "taking spells" when I needed her most. Even though my father worked out of town a lot and Mummy was left at home without a car nor much money, she found a way to get to the hospital every day to visit me and correspond with the doctor. Mummy would always look so beautiful when she came to see me, all dressed up complete with high-heels which I could hear clip-clopping down the hall. How I loved the sound of those heels getting closer and closer to my room. Sometimes she'd even bring me a little something from the gift shop. Looking back now, I have no idea how she afforded such trivial luxu-

ries. Nevertheless, my mother was there for me faithfully and God granted her strength to fulfill my needs... Much later in years we discovered some anti-convulsant drugs which greatly helped, but she told most outsiders the drug was simply for her migraine headaches. At this young age of nine I painfully learned that bad things can happen even as you pray. Watching and feeling Mummy having a seizure while lying right there beside me was acutely frightening yet, it made me realize I was all she had in that room and God was the one common denominator we both had. It never occurred to me even as a child to be mad at God for this; only how to be strong and responsible and how to return some of the love back to my mother.

If you pick a flower, give a flower. God gives us beauty to pass it on to others.

Ever notice how some people seem to prosper despite their poor environment and struggling conditions? I believe one doesn't necessarily require optimum opportunities to succeed. All one really needs is some patience, discipline, and endurance. This brings to mind an analogy I made with a single wildflower. I was walking along a busy sidewalk when I noticed a pretty flower sprouting up from almost solid concrete. Looking closer I found it had rooted itself in a small, circular opening about the size of a 50 cent piece. I suppose the hole used to support a

parking meter or trash receptacle. I thought long and hard about that unique wildflower. Regardless of the deficient soil, and the absence of any other flowers around, this tiny seed actually flourished. It was standing up very proud and perky as if to say: "Look what I've become even though the odds were against me"!

I don't know why, but I still get shocked and amazed at the many ways God presents Himself in my life. My sister and I spent hours upon hours in a small waiting room at the hospital waiting for either word from a doctor regarding Mother's latest surgery or just awaiting the next allowed visit with her. Anyhow, in the hallway just outside our little refuge, there were two soda vending machines. The front of the machines were similar as to how they appealed to the consumer. They were brightly colored, one blue, one red, and each had a picture of their soft drinks displayed in large cubes of crushed ice. This image covered almost the entire front surfaces of the large vending machines. Well, in order to pass the time Janie and I stared at the machines until we'd find a hidden picture. The pictures weren't put there intentionally, but it was kind of like seeing a certain image in a puffy cloud. Once we studied them long enough we deciphered a fish, a rabbit, a heart, and a mushroom. Then I thought I bet you God is watching us from here, and sure enough, when I looked long and hard for Him, there He was, so clearly that Janie was quickly able to seek Him out also.

I've always said my idea of world peace would be to walk down the main street of any major city at 2:00 a.m. without fear. Why don't we just make it happen? Sounds simple enough, right?

We can't be all things to all people at all times, but we can always be something to someone.

In baring my soul to all, this is the prayer I made up at age seven and have said it every night since...

Dear Heavenly Father, I pray to you through Thy son Jesus' name. I pray that you please be with my mother to keep her very safe, happy, and healthy. I pray that you be with all those who need your guidance to help and guide them. I pray for all those who are sick and in hospitals and those who are in sorrow to become happy again. I pray that you please be with all those who are handicapped, crippled, mentally retarded, misfortunate in any way such as these, Dear Lord. I pray that you please be with them all to give them something and someone to hold onto and to be there for them to help and brighten up their futures. All these things I ask in Thy precious name who has taught me to say as I pray; (Followed by the Lord's Prayer)

I've never before revealed my homemade invocation. Not even to my closest of close confidants. But now, I don't mind telling the world how I started my relationship with God. I always made addendums to adapt it

to my most current concerns and gratifications but, it remained my nightly format of prayer.

Eulogy given by Joni at her Mom's Funeral

It is impossible to put down on paper the love our family has for our dear, sweet mother. She was definitely one of a kind and we have many precious memories of her and how self-sacrificing she was. We never called her Mom or Mommy, she was always "Mummy." Looking back now it seems as though we had two different Mummy's in physical condition, but still the same in spirit. We had one before November 5, 1997, and one after November 5, 1997. The Mummy before was soft-spoken and rather inward. She had a great compassion for animals, nature, and music. She had an unusual, unique, keen sense of humor that only those closest to her could relate to, and she gave everyone she knew a nickname. She never was a socialite. She didn't know what it was like to go to bingo or card club, and she preferred catalog shopping from home over mall shopping, usually buying something for her children and grandchildren. As a matter of fact, she could never understand why people chose to go out and socialize when they could just as well stay home with their families. Growing up we had very little, but Mummy was such a sacrificer that we had everything we really needed from nothing. She thought nothing of wearing holey socks and nightgowns so that we could have pretty school clothes. Though they may not have been numerous, we had clothes that were clean and presentable. She hated whites that were not white and above all dirty shoelaces. She

instilled in us at a very young age to attend church. We were encouraged to go to Sunday school as children even if she had only a dime for us to put in the collection plate. Beauty came to her easily and without effort. She was always the prettiest, youngest mother of all. I didn't realize it until I was an adult that her beauty went so far beyond skin deep. Our Mummy after November 5, 1997, was so much stronger than we could have every imagined. Amidst all her medical disasters all of her vital organs kept right on pumping, functioning, expanding and contracting and that big heart of hers kept right on beating. The past four and a half years with her have been a constant up and down emotional roller coaster, but the good moments far outweighed the bad. Caring for her and allowing her to become completely dependent on us has been the best thing my family and I could have ever done with our lives. During the past four years after Mummy's brain surgery my sister and I were so grateful that she recovered most of her long-term memory. Our fondest moments are when we'd get into bed for the night. Mummy was her calmest and most talkative. She was so content after giving her husband a kiss goodnight and then falling asleep while reminiscing and holding our hand. The common thread between our two mothers was that she loved her family unconditionally, without fail and without question. It was so satisfying to grow up knowing her love was just always there. She'd never judge us or condemn us and she usually blamed herself when we faltered. Mummy, we thank you for being ours and we thank you for

devoting your life to us. We'll miss you every day, but God is ready for you. You once said, "Please promise me you won't worry when the Lord comes for me because I'll be ready." Even though you were unable to walk for the past four and one half years down here, we're sure that up in heaven you're walking tall. You'll be caring for all the animals and flowers and who knows...maybe someone up there could use a good nurse. Thank you for teaching us how to sacrifice as you did right up until your final days when you gave up your life to make room for your new great granddaughter. Hannah Jane thanks you and will be forever blessed to have been a part of you. We thank you, God, for lending her to us for the past 70 years.

Thank You note after mother's birthday party

A Mother's Love

A mother's love is like the wing of a bird,
Gently and gradually soaring high without a single word.
She treats me like the royalty of a great king or queen,
And doesn't think twice about forgiveness as she wipes my slate clean.
I always know her love is there, plentiful and deep as a well,
It spans far and wide like a rainbow but funny, how the colors never pale.
Her unconditional love is like my Holy Spirit,
Always there to call on but at times, I don't hear it.
The exalted feeling she gives me is like no other,
It can never be duplicated because we only get one mother.
I wonder, how can I repay her for all this love she gives?
I know only to say, "Thank You" each day that she lives.
She never tests my love or makes me fight for more,
I just know it's there and I'm what she's been living for.

Enclosure in mother's memory cards after the funeral

Thank you for sharing your time, love, and kindness in hopes that you just
may lighten our hearts,
We hold on so tightly to our loved ones it seems unfair when they do depart.
You did indeed show us that our mother was loved by many,
You gave, you prayed, you touched, for that time you put her above any.
Thank you for coming to us so lovingly to ease the pain that final day,
Though we wanted her for ourselves forever, here, she could not stay.
For our mother is also loved very much by her creator, God,
We realize we had to give her back, all He had to do was nod . . .

Thank you for sharing our love.

I learned a very beneficial tip from my publisher that I'd like to pass on to everyone. It is so simple, yet so deep. At the outset of my writing career I assumed there were countless rules and tricks to the trade. When I sit down to write, I can deliver page after page of thoughts because they are "just in my head"! However, having no journalistic background, of course, I was concerned about the proper format, how to spice everything up with colorful terminology, and using correct punctuation. That was when Tom enlightened me with these three modest words, "less is more."

Boy has that tiny phrase been a blessing. It is so true. One doesn't need fancy words to skirt around true-to-life stories. Thoughts seem to be so much more moving when they are relatable and easy to comprehend. I know myself that a statement kind of loses some of its impact if I have to pull out the dictionary with every other page. It is a good thing to expand one's vocabulary (don't get me wrong, I enjoy learning new words), but I agree with Tom. When you want to send a sincere message from the heart, less is more!

A tribute to the Publisher…

A whole sky-full of "thank you's" to my publisher, Tom Costello. When I first contacted Tom by phone he was very professional, but warm. However, when I briefed him on my project he was less than encouraging. He adamantly stated that he was extremely busy and very particular about the types of books he published. He said he had just gotten off the phone with a lady regarding her poetry. He simply told her, in his opinion, it was not going to sell. He had previously attempted to convince her during a three-hour-long meeting that her work just wasn't one with which he felt good about becoming involved. Well, as you can imagine, I, as a total novice, was certain I would be wasting my time with Mr. Costello. Do you think I would take heed to my inclinations and refine my approach and presentation? Noooooo, of course not. So here I go, off the very next day to this very polished, prominent, Mr. Big Time Author/ Publisher. I have in hand only a badly wrinkled, scribbled up manila envelope. Suddenly, it hit me: Joni, are you nuts? Nothing was in any semblance of order; everything was completely haphazard, just a pile of scraps of paper. Some were hand written, some typed, on all different kinds of paper. I remember there was even a napkin with some chicken scratch on it. I desperately wanted to rewind a day and go back to post phone conversation. Why didn't I at least somewhat organize my precious manuscript? Now he knew; I definitely was there taking up his

valuable time. I only wondered how he was going to be able to let me down gently since I was already privy to his encounter with the poetry lady. Then I noticed he was actually shuffling through the rubble and, now, he had half a smile on his face while he read some of the tattered papers. He looked up and said, "I love it; I'll do it"!!! Can you imagine my joy after having gone through so many months of bad news, dim outlooks, and poor prognoses? Tom and I founded a friendship that afternoon. He has been such an inspiration to me as a first-time, no-name author. He is a real person and a decent human being first and a business-man second. I thank you, Tom, from the bottom of my heart for always subtly guiding me in the right direction and for being my friend.

Reading the words of Joni Carol is...
like returning to an old friend for advice and comfort and quiet wisdom and finding it again. Her voice is reassuring and her observations about life and nature and people are those of someone with a caring and keen eye and ear. It is impossible not to like and be warmed by the glow of the woman talking and reminding and showing and questioning...I think people who come to this book seeking any kind of help or guidance or hope are going to come away from it feeling better about themselves and their problems, and in general feeling refreshed about life.

Tom Costello, publisher

Dear Joni, I have just finished reading your book. I am still crying! You Joni, have a love that is unconditional. The world should have more people with your compassion and devotion. You and Janie are the only ones who have kept our mother alive. If she were to pass tomorrow, she has had more love than anyone could ever dream of. For that you deserve the highest medal awarded, if there is such a thing. I am so proud of you. The tears continually roll down my face. You have given more to the world than most people could ever comprehend. You truly are the "sunshine" you write about. IIIIIIIIIIIIIIIIIII Loveeeeeeee Youuuuuuuu,

Your number one fan, Brother Markie
Vallejo, California

About the Author

Joni Carol is a 46-year-old part-time writer, full time dental office manager, and care giver to her mother. She was driven to write this book after her mother's very complex medical disaster and on-going recovery. Her mother, a 66-year-old retired nurse, walked into the hospital on November 5, 1997, and left by wheelchair on March 25, 1998, to become a resident at a nursing home. The hospital stay started with a massive cerebral hemorrhage, then two incidents of spinal meningitis. Just when they thought they saw that proverbial light at the end of the tunnel, she was smittened with acute peritonitis. All vital organs were septic, and again there was little hope. The small progress she had made was negated. She then nearly had her foot amputated due to blood clots and almost lost an arm due to extreme I.V. infiltration. Joni and her sister, a two-man army, rotated shifts to stand vigil at her bedside night and day or as much as allowed by hospital policy. For three days the hospital staff permitted them free access to the ICU, day or night. Normal policy is three, one hour scheduled visits throughout the day. They allowed this because they were convinced every next breath was going to be her last. Their mother's main attending nurse even requested to be removed from her

case, as her condition was just too heart-rendering for the nurse to bear. No matter how bleak the outlook was, Joni never gave up hope. She inhaled every positive fragment that came her way. Even the most trivial of comments, either written or spoken, linger on, still, in her mind. Close friends, strangers, daily contact people and her inner spirit all lent encouragement along the way to inspire her. Joni wrote this book in an effort to reach out to others in dire emotional distress. She asks that you please clutch tight to all the beauty in the world around us. Don't allow darkness to overshadow your sun for long. She believes good things truly do result from bad things.

After reading your book I made it mandatory reading for my entire office staff.

Dr. James T. Cole, Chiropractor
West Newton, Pennsylvania

Joni, I need to say more about your book, which is to say, more about you. Unique, genuine, sincere, wise, balanced, not preachy, from your heart to my heart. It is also brief and can be easily carried about, read at bedside, or stoplights. Just morsels to think of, and, sunshine on a cloudy day. To be honest, there are people who write to have written. You seem to write just to express and help others by sharing your pure heart and experience.

Father James Becherer
Sheffield Lake, Ohio

Once I started reading her book, I couldn't stop, as her real-life story of medical misfortune is buoyed by insights that can help others through troubled times.

David Templeton , Newspaper Reporter
Pittsburgh Post Gazette, Pennsylvania

Joni, I just read something from your book and, it helps me to get through the day, every day!

Beverly Niccolai, Artist
Belle Vernon, Pennsylvania

Joni, I started reading your book as soon as I got off work. I was sitting in the parking lot waiting for the car to warm up. Before I knew it, I'd been reading for 35 minutes, still sitting in the parking lot!!! I was in tears while reading this beautiful work! What a true inspiration you are! I can feel everything you wrote and felt. I truly know about the sunshine and I am grateful for every moment, both good and bad! Thank you for this beautiful reminder so that I can share it with others.

Rose Hinson, USAirways Ticket Agent
Charlotte, North Carolina

Joni, I have just finished your book. I wish I could memorize it so that it would become the first source of my reaction to day to day life. It is so reflective of the way Christ taught us to live. I could hear your voice and see your smile as I read the words. Your book filled me with respect for you and your family. In this time of great tragedy in our country your words could comfort so many.

[written 09-14-01]   Luann Daugherty,
Retired Political Executive Secretary
Monongahela, Pennsylvania